POLICE OPERATIONAL INTELLIGENCE

(Revised Second Printing)

POLICE OPERATIONAL INTELLIGENCE

By

DONALD O. SCHULTZ, B.S., M.P.A.

Police Instructor, Broward Community College
Fort Lauderdale, Florida

and

LORAN A. NORTON, B.S.

Lieutenant, Santa Ana Police Department
Santa Ana, California

CHARLES C THOMAS · PUBLISHER
Springfield · *Illinois* · *U.S.A.*

Published and Distributed Throughout the World by
CHARLES C THOMAS • PUBLISHER
BANNERSTONE HOUSE
301-327 East Lawrence Avenue, Springfield, Illinois, U.S.A.
NATCHEZ PLANTATION HOUSE
735 North Atlantic Boulevard, Fort Lauderdale, Florida, U.S.A.

First Printing, 1968
Revised Second Printing, 1971

With THOMAS BOOKS *careful attention is given to all details of manufacturing and design. It is the Publisher's desire to present books that are satisfactory as to their physical qualities and artistic possibilities and appropriate for their particular use. THOMAS BOOKS will be true to those laws of quality that assure a good name and good will.*

Printed in the United States of America
EE–16

DEDICATION

To the giants of the police intelligence community, J. Edgar Hoover, Director of the Federal Bureau of Investigation; the late William Parker, Chief, Los Angeles Police Department; and that intelligence officer who gave his life in the pursuit of law and order.

INTRODUCTION

THE effectiveness of the administration of any law enforcement agency depends, in part, upon its ability to obtain, process, and utilize critical intelligence information. The late William Parker, Chief of the Los Angeles Police Department, one of the giants of the Police Intelligence Community, once said, "Against organized crime, Internal Affairs is my defensive arm; Intelligence is my offensive arm."

Many misunderstandings exist in the minds of different police administrators regarding what intelligence really is. Police operational intelligence is simply the gathering and processing of information. It is not a magic formula that will resolve all the problems that may be encountered by the Police Administrator. Fundamentally stated, its purpose is to increase the probability of accuracy in operational staff decisions.

Too often, Police Administrators are required to make major decisions based upon inadequate information. The function of intelligence is to fill the void which often exists in police decision-making. The intelligence unit is not an internal affairs disciplinary section. In a sense, it can be said that it is the investigative arm of the planner.

As organized crime and militant organizations continue their infiltration into the American way of life, municipal law enforcement will be compelled to develop tools which are necessary to combat the alien efforts. In theory, intelligence, in one sense of the word, provides a greater focus on those criminal activities that generally go unnoticed until such time as they have evolved into a major community problem. In this sense intelligence has a preventative aspect.

The future appears to reflect that the "Intelligence Community" within municipal law enforcement will continue to grow. Traditional methods are not the answer to combatting organized crime and subversive activities. Research in such fields as sociology, psychology, and data processing are entering the law enforcement field. By example, police data processing techniques of the next decade will be revolutionary. Intelligence capabilities will grow geometrically with each new generation of computers.

It is the purpose of this text to develop a generally broader understanding of the intelligence concepts as they apply to law enforcement, and to assist in the development of a greater appreciation for the need for a more widespread "Intelligence Community" with the law enforcement profession.

This text should not be viewed as a technical operating manual for the intelligence unit. It is a compilation designed to acquaint the layman and embryo officer with a better understanding of the role of intelligence in the law enforcement field.

PREFACE

Most intelligence activities are popularly misconstrued as being a secret group conducting clandestine activities. This is not the case. Intelligence is hard work, involving the gathering and filtering of great volumes of data.

The patrol division of the modern police agency is often referred to as the "workhorse" or the "backbone" of the department. We can just as appropriately say that intelligence is the "nerve center" that gives the proper attuning to the enforcement anatomy.

The future appears to hold great promise for the intelligence service within the municipal law enforcement community. The advent of fourth and fifth generation computers and other technology, coupled with the advances in sociology, psychology, and criminology, indicates that policemen are about to step from the shadows of the dark ages.

Regardless of the questionable restrictions being imposed upon law enforcement, plus the weight of tradition, the coming applications of science and industry will revolutionize the police science field. The crime prevention aspects and predictions of police operational intelligence will play a significant role.

In the preparation of this text, we borrowed materials from many different sources, authors and investigators with intelligence experience. To our knowledge, this text book is a first in the field of municipal police intelligence activities. Undoubtedly, there are many men presently working in this field who are as well qualified to write this text. It is our hope that they will soon contribute to this body of knowledge by writing similar material.

ACKNOWLEDGMENTS

THE authors gratefully acknowledge the assistance and cooperation received from the following people and organizations: J. Edgar Hoover, Director of the Federal Bureau of Investigation; Henry Reining Jr., Ph.D., Dean and Professor of Public Administration, University of Southern California; Joel Hayes, Chief Investigator, Orange County District Attorney's Office, Santa Ana, California; William Farr, Register Staff Reporter, Santa Ana, California; Dino D. Caiazzi, Investigator, Vice and Narcotic Division, Santa Ana Police Department, Santa Ana, California; Gene Tucker, artist extraordinary and friend of law enforcement; IBM Corporation, Armonk, New York; and the Intelligence Division, Los Angeles Police Department, Los Angeles, California.

D.O.S.
L.A.N.

CONTENTS

POLICE OPERATIONAL INTELLIGENCE

HISTORY OF INTELLIGENCE

What to look for in this chapter...

The beginning of military intelligence;
Some of the historical highlights of military intelligence;
The early development of the police service and their intelligence activities;
The beginning of LEIU.

MILITARY INTELLIGENCE

T HE incalculable misery and suffering brought to good men and women from every walk of life, as a result of organized criminal schemes, would cause even the most seasoned lawman to give the hue and cry if he knew only a small part of the total picture. General apathy and traditional police thinking have had a crushing effect on the formal development of a tool necessary to neutralize or eliminate the effects of the illegal corporations who prey on the weakness of man.

As we delve into the past, let us borrow and paraphrase a bit. Those nations or civilizations which fail to profit from history's errors are doomed to repeat them. Most municipal police organizations in the United States are repeating the same errors that they made fifty years ago. Many times more often than necessary, police administrators lack sufficient intelligence data essential to effective planning.

The history of police and military intelligence provides some interesting insights, for it appears that only rarely does an untried intelligence concept come along. The artful employers of intelligence agents have been legion. We could never possibly count them all, and probably, the greatest of them are unknown to history. Historians, in their "great-man" treatment of history have somewhat neglected the commanders of the secret, invisible

3

army of intelligence agents which have had a profound effect on the course of events.

Moses

One of the first recorded formalized intelligence efforts, with format, can be found in the Holy Bible (Numbers 13:17) :

> And Moses sent them to spy out the land of Canaan, and Said unto them, Get you up this way southward, and go up into the mountain;
> And see the land, what it is; and the people that dwelleth therein, whether they be strong or weak, few or many;
> And what the land is that they dwell in, whether it be good or bad; and what cities they be that they dwell in, whether in tents, or in strongholds; and what the land is, whether it be fat or lean, whether there be wood therein, or not. An be ye of good courage and bring of the fruit of the land. Now the time was the time of the first ripe grapes.

The Scriptures also named the twelve intelligence agents whom the Lord directed Moses to send into the land of Canaan (Numbers 13:3-15) and records that "all those men were heads of the children of Israel." When Moses sent them north, to spy out the land, he did not propose a mere topographical expedition or cursory exploration.

Had Moses distributed his twelve intelligence agents as a cross-country chain, with each one dependent upon the cooperation of his eleven associates, we would be able to trace the origin of organized and systematic intelligence from its earliest environment. The biblical record, however, is clear; the instructions to the intelligence agents of Israel show that they formed an espionage duplicated a dozen times to allow for the probabilities of discovery and death.

Rehab

Rehab, the harlot of Jericho (Joshua 2:1-21) who sheltered and concealed the agents of Israel, made a covenant with the agents and duped their pursuers. She was not only an impromptu confederate of immense value to the Jewish leaders of that far-distant day, but also established a plot-pattern which is still of periodic relief to motion-picture producers.

Delilah

Delilah was an impromptu intelligence agent of the Philistines. Apart from her tonsorial specialty, she allowed Philistine spies to hide in her house (Judges, 16:9) and used her sex to gain intelligence from a powerful enemy. She achieved what amounted to a complete intelligence triumph, locating the largest effective force of her employers' adversaries and contriving the stroke which put that force out of action.

Alexander the Great

The necessities of compression and the complexities of more modern intelligence services draw us rapidly down the earlier centuries. When Alexander the Great was marching into Asia, it is recorded there came to him hints, and rumors of disaffection growing among his allies and mercenaries. The young conqueror thereupon sought the truth and got it by the simplest expedient. He announced that he was writing home and recommended to his officers that they do likewise. Then, when the couriers were ladened and had set out for Greece, he ordered them quietly recalled and proceeded to investigate all the letters that they carried. Malcontents were detected; legitimate causes of grievance exposed.

Sertorius

When Sertorius was the Roman Commander in Spain he was, according to Polyaenus, the possessor of a white fawn that he had trained to follow him everywhere. ". . . even to the steps of the tribunal." This little fawn was taught to approach at a given signal, and Sertorius himself gave the signal, when about to pronounce his decision in judicial cases. The fawn appeared to convey information to the Roman general; and Sertorius allowed it to become widely known that he derived both secrets and guidance from the fawn. His intelligence agents meanwhile, were everywhere active, and all that they learned was credited to the supernatural powers of the animal.

Crassus of Rome

History does not omit that some would discover the profit they might gain from a private system of intelligence agents.

The man who made the discovery and put it into execution with striking and grimly humorous results was Marcus Lucinius Crassus of Rome. The intelligence service of Crassus was well organized and skillfully operated; it not only excelled the espionage of its contemporaries but is by far the best of its kind to be found in the annals of antiquity.

Crassus, employing both slaves and freemen, next organized a complicated enterprise which seems the only case on record wherein a millionaire became a multimillionaire by combining private intelligence agents with a private fire brigade. This fire-fighting contingent was perhaps the most ironically humorous of all the many "rackets" devised by Roman speculators. Five hundred workmen, equipped with ropes, buckets, ladders and other implements, were held in readiness until one of Crassus' roving agents' tapped his widespread communicative system and reported a fire. The crowded, unsanitary conditions of ancient cities made fires both frequent and dangerous. Crassus, given an alarm to answer, would rally forth at the head of his salvage corps, approach the neighborhood of the fire, see which way the wind was blowing, and begin interviewing householders whose property seemed most endangered. He would offer to buy their houses, as they stood, for an unreasonably low price. If the frightened owner agreed, the fire brigade was hurried into action and generally managed to save the property. If the owner kept his head and refused to be taken advantage of, Crassus trooped off with his firemen, leaving the blaze as a public responsibility. In time, according to Plutarch, he became master of a very considerable part of the house property of Rome.

The intelligence operatives of Crassus, when not objectively looking for fires, were devoted in the main to gathering evidence for Crassus to use in the law courts. Crassus thus became a kind of underworld power as well as a plutocrat.

Akbar

By means of remarkably devised operations of intelligence, the Mongul emperors of India regulated a vast and populous realm having the utmost social and religious complexity. Akbar as the "Great Mogul," with no pressing anxiety about his neighbors or interest in espionage beyond his own frontiers, this sagacious master of Hindustan employed more than four thousand agents for the sole purpose of bringing him the truth that his throne might rest upon it.

Genghis Khan

The Golden Emperor of Cathay unwisely asked Genghis Khan for Mongol aid in his continual war upon the ancient house of Sung in South China. Chepe Noyon, ". . . with his weakness for wearing sable boots" was sent with a force of calvalry to fight beside the Cathayans while closely observing the riches of their land. Soon after the return of this intelligence expedition Genghis Khan began preparing to invade Cathay. This was his first attempt upon a civilized power of superior defensive strength, and even now he launched his campaign by dispatching beyond the great wall a contingent of spies and scouts, who were "to capture and bring back informers." Espionage and artifice had a vital part in the Mongols conquest of China.

Frederick the Great

Frederick the Great, father of organized military espionage, has been quoted as saying that he had, when in the field, one cook and a hundred agents. It was his habit to divide his agents into four classes (a) common spies recruited among poor folk, glad to earn a small sum or to accommodate a military officer; (b) double spies, the low informers and unreliable renegades of value chiefly in spreading false information to the enemy; (c) spies of consequence—courtiers and noblemen, staff officers and kindred conspirators, invariably requiring a substantial bribe or bait; and (d) persons who are forced to undertake espionage against their will. The energetic Prussian did more than classify, he established rules for obtaining and using every grade of spy or intelligence agent.

Under his fourth category he suggested that a rich burgher must be thoroughly intimidated which might best be done with threats to burn down his home, destroy his fortune, or injure or even kill his wife and children. The burgher, a good man of peace and local repute, one who had been properly molded by his anxiety, could be made to serve by accompanying a trained military agent into the camp of the enemy, where his appearance, reputation, and character would mask the real spy's activities. Despite his forced labor of pretense, the burgher could be relied upon to behave amiably enough if often reminded that members of his family were the hostages held by those to whom the real spy, his companion, would report at the conclusion of their joint espionage venture.

Frederick's four classifications overlooked the modern patriot spy. The Prussian was a realist, a cynic and an absolute monarch. Reigning sovereigns of his day were seldom in touch with genuine patriotism. The French revolution had yet to fire Europe with nationalist enthusiasms. Threats and bribes, promises of promotion and gain, were the inducements that the spy-masters of Frederick's school understood how to use.

Hannibal

Hannibal's invasion of Italy, the most brilliant and futile raid in history, gained him many victories and nearly bled Rome to death, but the mere slaughter of Romans and a great city's despair would not have sustained him for fifteen years if he had not also made powerful allies and developed an excellent intelligence system. (He often dressed as a beggar and went into the streets of Rome.)

Spanish Inquisition

Frey Tomas de Torquenmada, the Dominican monk who became grand inquisitor, was the principal architect of the hideous Spanish Inquisition. This Chekist of the Holy Church—whose authority came to him by royal edict, dated September 27, 1480 —not only put his demonic imprint upon the life and religious thought of Spain for generations to come, but also bequested modern government a pattern which no master of political police need ever attempt to excel.

The Inquisition not only relied upon espionage, but also trained its corps of intelligence agents carefully and well, issuing a manual for their guidance which was as candid and unblushing about the technique of betrayal as the manuals issued to its inquisitors were disingenuous, diabolical, and blandly barbarous. There is a "compendious tone" annotated by Francesco Pegna, first published in Rome, 1585, that preserves for us, among many stratagems, this classic admonition of church espionage.

Politicians of the Holy Roman Empire and of the even holier Roman Catholic Church employed spies, disbursed bribes and fomented pretentious conspiracies. The great campaigns of ecclesiastical secret service managed by the Inquisition, the Jesuits, and other instruments heated and sharpened to harry the infidel or heretic, are unparalleled. (Juan Antonio Llorento records this with completeness in *Historia Critica de la Inquisician de Espana*.)

Jesuits

It is not inappropriate to call the Jesuits "shock troops" in their intelligence missions as well as in their better-known work as spiritual missionaries and teachers of the Catholic faith. The Jesuits proved themselves the cleverest and most energetic of workers for the Catholic cause. Perhaps the populace must be stirred up against a king of independent faith, or some natural exercise of secular powers seemed inconvenient to the politicians of the church. Jesuit fathers were the agents for such an ecclesiastical emergency.

Not too many years after the printing press was invented, two of the more formidable agents of the Church of Rome, Jesuits, Robert Parsons and Edmund Campion were found to have set up a secret printing press at Stonors Park near Henley. Clandestine publications have since then become a standard agency of offensive intelligence agents.

State Informer

One of the earliest efforts to establish systematic police was the so-called Watch and Ward statute of Edward I, in 1285, which recognized the principle that inhabitants of every district must combine for their own protection against the lawless. By royal proclamation the profession of "State Informer" was created in 1434. What the informer was particularly enjoined to discover and expose was the writing, distributing or affixing of seditious bills. The reward of the informer in such cases (twenty pounds and one half of the goods of the convicted seditionist) was a substantial gain, which probably invited much trafficking in false information.

Walsingham of England

English history reflects the intelligence service achievements of Walsingham were great because his adversaries were numerous, implacable and filled with murderous zeal. He protected Queen Elizabeth I from countless assassins. Walsingham's best agents were English students residing in Italy. Walsingham gave England its first national "secret service." Largely guided by Walsingham, the English government made a shrewd attempt to retard the sailing of the Armada, whose exact condition of offensive readiness was so accurately divulged to London. Bankers of Genoa were induced to withhold loans to Philip II, so that in addition to the knowledge which is power, the power that was golden ducats also came to be delicately manipulated by English intelligence.

Fouché of France

Joseph Fouché, a Frenchman, born in 1759, in Pellerin, near the seaport town of Nantes, rose to become one of the most feared and most respected intelligence directors in the history of France. Rising to become Minister of Police and defeating Robespierre in the battles of intrigue, Fouché created a network of agents that knew almost everything anyone did or was about to do. Fouché's assistant, Desmarest, invented the modern system of spying on spies, which honors its originators with its generally accepted French title, "contre-espionnage." They often made use of a disreputable device, the "Test of Fidelity." Each potential agent had to provide them with a permanent hold upon him by committing some "directed" crime at the outset. Evidence of this compulsory felony was then preserved with the other documents relating to the case and, if need be, found useful in discrediting him with any friends, or other affairs of discipline and control.

Fouché undoubtedly had a definite influence upon the history of France; Napoleon was constantly attuned to the intelligence data acquired by Fouché.

Schulmeister, Napoleon's Eyes

Karl Schulmeister, who is the Napoleon of military secret service, born on August 5, 1770 in Neu-Freistett, was the son of an unattached Lutheran clergyman. Schulmeister was an accomplished and popular smuggler—or contrabandist, as he described himself, at the age of seventeen.

Napoleon's campaign in 1805 against Austria and Russia was a perfectly timed and maneuvered military masterpiece. Schulmeister began his career in offensive espionage during this same campaign. Napoleon had always endeavored to study the character of the generals his royal foes selected to defeat him. In 1805, Austrian hopes rested upon Marshal Mack.

Karl Schulmeister, the spy, first appeared in Vienna in a cover role as a young man of noble Hungarian ancestry, lately exiled from France after many years residence because Napoleon suspected him of spying for Austria. Mack, after interviewing the alleged exile, was impressed by all that he seemed to know about the civil and military conditions of France and gladly availed himself of such fortuitous espionage. The spy became his protege and was introduced by him into the exclusive army clubs of Vienna. Mack even obtained a commission and attached him to his personal staff. In the fateful autumn of 1805, they took the field together. Schulmeister, the spy, serving as the Austrian's Chief of Intelligence, was worth more than an army of Napoleon.

This was the beginning of the end of Mack's military career. Marshal Mack was deprived of his rank, disgraced and imprisoned until his betrayal could be established by his friends.

Schulmeister was aided, in his endeavor against the Austrian military machine, by Napoleon, who provided him with fictitious newspapers which were printed to reinforce the false data that Schulmeister had given to Marshal Mack. Though Schulmeister died a poor man, his intelligence accomplishments for Napoleon rank with some of the most worthy achievements of military conquest.

Washington

Conspirators under oath abound in the history of every nation. It is probable that there has been a drop of blood pricked out to form a signature upon some clandestine parchment or manifesto for every drop shed in the greatest battle known to medieval or modern times. Whenever a genuine secret society has turned to secular or political activities, it has achieved significant results. George Washington as grand master mobilized the Freemasons of the colonies at the outbreak of the American War of Independence.

Carbonari

The impression which resulted—of the Freemasons as potential insurgents—has survived to this day in certain states of Europe, notably Italy. The dread instilled by oaths of banded brotherhood derives from the insurrectionary endeavors of the Italian Carbonari. It is widely conceded that the Carbonari branched off from the Masonic order. They cherished the most patriotic of motives, most of them were noble in conspiracy and disinterested as revolutionists.

The Carbonari never weighted themselves seriously with a governing program. They never got around to agreeing upon what particular form of government they would set up when and if they succeeded in overthrowing the existing authority. One viewing them sympathetically from this time perspective cannot escape the suspicion that succeeding was not their paramount concern, that they cared for no program save their zestful plots and fermentations, and that belligerent opposition to the tyrant was their sole, and thoroughly satisfying, reward.

The secret society enrolled nobles, army officers, small landlords, government officials, peasants and even a few priests. Its organization was one of the curiosities of the age. Its ritual was a fantastic composition of symbols borrowed from the Christian religion and from the trade of charcoal-burning, so extensively practiced in the mountains of Calabria and the Abruzzi. A carbonarist lodge was termed a vendita (sale) and its members saluted one another as "good cousins," *buoni cugini*.

Camorra and Mafia

It was no new thing to find a criminal element weighing heavily in Italian politics. If in our own day, one man has succeeded in pocketing politics, he initiated his drive by molding organized lawless elements into a secret police. The most complete criminal organizations known to Italian history were the Mafia and the Camorra. The former was a Sicilian order, presumed to trace its ancestry to a local cell of the Camorra.

The Camorra, an association at least four centuries old, had originated in the Neapolitan prisons where, upon the pretext of keeping a lamp alight before a prison shrine, a tax was levied upon all newcomers. The extortions of the Camorra were not long confined to inmates of jails. Probationers, who had to attend to assassinations and pass other tests for a term of years, only shared in the society's loot as they proved they could both enforce and endure its discipline. From the "sala," or small slice, one advanced to the "barattalo," or half shares, in time, the full share, or "camorra" was bestowed upon those sufficiently lawless, daring and vengeful.

Stieber

No historical account of intelligence could fairly neglect to mention the Prussian master, Wilhelm Stieber. His exploits in military intelligence probably set the pattern that the European nations followed for decades to come. Intelligence was deemed a necessary general staff support system.

Stieber, early in youth was scheduled for the Lutheran ministry, but ultimately dodged into the legal profession, where he turned almost immediately to criminal cases. In not too many years he became Minister of Police. Stieber left the police service to become an intelligence agent for Bismarck, who later labeled him the "King of sleuth-hounds." During this time Stieber made two major contributions to the science of military intelligence, namely military censorship and organized military propaganda. His exploits in France gathering data regarding French readiness for war are an example of the value of a highly trained intelligence agent. Working as a census taker, Stieber developed an informal format which included everything which struck him as likely to expedite an invasion or provide for the invaders. This format, developed in approximately 1866-1870, is perhaps the most significant example of the modern intelligence approach which utilized statisticians, accounts, and, other men of the mathematical arts.

Redl

One of the most brilliant intelligence agents, though he was a homosexual, was Alfred Redl. Redl, coming from a comparatively poor family which had little social prominence, rose to become chief of the Austro-Hungarian Secret Service, or in other terms, director of their military intelligence system. For more than half of his time as director of intelligence, Redl was acting as an intelligence agent for Russia.

In 1913, proof of Redl's treason was discovered and shortly thereafter, Redl was compelled to commit suicide. The history of his thirteen-year episode as an arch spy, led to the deaths of over 500,000 agents and soldiers combined, in the military establishment.

Many Others

World War I and the related period contributed many names to the roll call of intelligence agents. Those who made major contributions are only few in number compared to those who were caught and executed or imprisoned. However, whether they died or not, a certain few had a considerable impact on the history of their countries and in some cases, upon the future of mankind. Wassmuss of Persia, Captain Von Rintelen, Mata Hari, Edith Canell, Alice Dubois, Captain M. Cumming, Colonel Lawrence, and Elisabeth Schragmiller, were by no means the only great agents. Space does not permit the recapitulation of their exploits, but one fact emerges, the military leaders of the various nations were beginning to formalize the intelligence activity and give it a much more important role in military affairs.

United States Military Intelligence

The United States was "slow to recognize the importance of military intelligence" as indicated in ROTC Manual 145-20, page 491. The Civil War records some interesting episodes of Allan Pinkerton, who was the first Chief of Secret Service.

Pinkerton weathered fairly well in the apprehension of criminals but was rather unsuccessful in intelligence matters (see *The Pinkerton Story*, G. P. Putnam, 1951, chapter 4.)

When the United States entered World War I, the intelligence community was probably smaller than the average American family and this excludes kin folk; however, by the war's end, this community approached approximately 1500 members. Peyton C. March in *Nation at War* (page 229) gives a good account of this.

Upon entry into World War II, the United States, comparatively speaking, was in little better condition than when entering World War I. General Eisenhower, on page 32 of *Crusade in Europe* relates:

> Our own feeble gesture in this direction was the maintenance of military attaches in most foreign capitals, and since public funds were not available to meet the unusual expenses of this type of duty, only officers with independent means could normally be detailed to these posts. Usually they were estimable, socially acceptable gentlemen; few knew the essentials of Intelligence work. Results were almost completely negative and the situation was not helped by the custom of making long service as a military attache, rather than ability, the essential qualification for appointment as head of the Intelligence Division in the War Department.

Donovan

Colonel William Donovan was directed by President Roosevelt to draft a plan for a new intelligence service approximately six months before the Japanese attack on Pearl Harbor. Donovan, who later rose to Major General, was in the process of organizing a national intelligence system, plus cutting red tape. Many authors of texts surrounding the Pearl Harbor attack hint that existing intelligence estimates indicated that the Japanese would not attack, yet, data were available to the contrary, but uncoordinated. Donovan in his work entitled *Intelligence: Key to Defense* relates that he had to start with almost nothing and build an entire coordinated national intelligence system. We are fortunate that he did not fear red tape.

Colonel Donovan, though never really achieving a central intelligence system, did develop the Office of Strategic Services

(OSS) whose exploits became almost legendary. Their successes and failures provided the necessary experience needed by the United States in her role as the leading nation of liberty.

Foreign political action, espionage, propaganda warfare, things which had been *previously frowned upon by* some of military leaders and congressmen, became standard items of hardware. The total activities of OSS called for a wide variety of skills and personalities. Problems of management, control, and security were compounded by intensive efforts of foreign intelligence agents, some friendly and some unfriendly. What could have been better, a foreign intelligence agent obtaining a position with OSS and eventually working to management level. Though no public knowledge of this is handy, history reflects that this is one of the most desirable targets of any intelligence system. It can ultimately be compared to playing chess with a deadman. A good example of this is recorded by Mieczyslau M. Nowinski, in "Behind Poland's Defeat" (*American Mercury,* April 1940).

> The defeat of Poland, how was it possible? The perfection of the German advance can only be explained by saying the Nazis were in possession of the most complete information about Polish plans and military secrets. The precision of the German Intelligence in Poland amazed even the leaders of the British Secret Service.
>
> When the war started the German General Staff knew more about the Polish Army than the majority of the Polish Generals.

During World War II, OSS was called upon to perform sometimes spectacular intelligence missions. On occasion their agents were parachuted into enemy countries to organize the underground movements (see "Jump-In to Adventure," *Readers Digest,* June 1945).

OSS agents working in conjunction with British Intelligence discovered Peenemunde which was the V-2 guided missile research project of Germany. Some people believe that Britain was saved and the war won by the six months delay that resulted from the early discovery and heavy bombing of Peenemunde (see "Forty Minutes that Changed the War," *Readers Digest,* October 1944.)

OSS agents not only gathered critical intelligence data, but also organized effective sabotage in most enemy industrial centers.

Also worthy of mention is the fact that the agents either directly or indirectly rescued more than five thousand American airmen, not to mention the communications network required to do this.

Probably their most significant accomplishments will never be made public. Many writers have hinted that some of their exploits critically affected the final outcome of the war in Europe. Perhaps history will someday pay tribute to this silent service, and give proper national recognition to the great American soldiers who walked this unique path in the defense of their country.

In October, 1945, President Truman disbanded the OSS, perhaps realizing that the United States did not in fact have a centralized intelligence service, or perhaps in an effort to keep peace with the Army, Navy, Air Force and State Department and their intelligence division.

A dispute developed over whether or not a national intelligence service should be highly centralized or not. In January, 1946, President Truman issued an Executive Order establishing the Central Intelligence Group (CIG), a compromise between the factions representing centralization and decentralization. The CIG operated under the control of the National Intelligence Authority (NIA) which was composed of the Secretaries of State, War, and Navy, plus a representative of the President.

CIA

The National Security Act of 1947 abolished CIG and NIA and unified the intelligence functions more closely under the National Security Council (NSC) and the Central Intelligence Agency (CIA). This act designated specific functions to be performed by CIA under the control of NSC. These functions related principally to advising NSC, after correlating and evaluating intelligence matters affecting national security. Outside of the United States the activities of CIA appear to be broader. (See Figure 1.1 For CIA and relationships to other intelligence agencies.)

Congress specifically limited CIA by excluding police powers and internal security functions. These functions were retained by the Federal Bureau of Investigation and other law enforcement agencies.

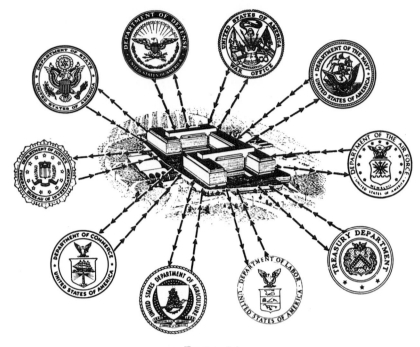

FIGURE 1.1.

Within CIA, the Director and his deputy are appointed by the President with the approval of the senate required. The personnel practices are under the control of the Director and are not subject to civil service. The Director also has wide latitude in funding various activities.

From a personnel standpoint, CIA enjoys a particular advantage in the military intelligence family in that officers within the military establishments are subjected to a rotation philosophy to "round out" their careers, or are rotated for some other reason or whim. CIA is and must be a career service for those who continue to qualify.

POLICE INTELLIGENCE

Where does a person begin a discussion of the past regarding police intelligence activity? Historically speaking, municipal police, excluding their intelligence services, are still in infancy compared to military experience. Intelligence activities of police in Europe, even today, are somewhat intertwined with the political and military establishments. A brief examination of the history of law enforcement offers little in regard to the formalization of one of its components, police operational intelligence.

The Holy Bible (Acts 22:4) relates that Paul had been given the power of arrest and commitment by the priests and elders. Law enforcement of this day seemed to be by mandate of the elders and religious leaders.

Two thousand years or so before the birth of Christ, Hammurabi, the King of Babylon, codified a set of rules and penalties for transactions among his subjects. Messengers delivered and carried out the law and the affixed penalties.

Some five hundred years after Hammurabi, the Egyptians, along with advancements in medicine, developed a court system. Custom houses on the Nile Delta also indicated police regulation. This may have been one of the first attempts to regulate goods coming into a country.

Greek city states, particularly Athens and Sparta, employed guards for the wall towers and for the person of the ruler. The ruler usually had a police force to keep him informed of court intrigue.

Perhaps the greatest contribution that ancient Rome gave to the modern world was her laws. The "Vigiles" of Rome were perhaps the first non-military law enforcement group. Though law enforcement was not their sole duty, they were armed with various weapons and were principally responsible for maintaining peace in the city.

Early England

When Rome fell, the recording of history also fell. Little is available until the seventh and eighth century in France and England. The English countryside became dotted with "Tuns" (towns) with the "hue and cry" as the means of apprehending offenders.

As the population of England expanded, the "Tithing system" developed in which people were grouped in ten families for the assumption of responsibility for law and order. Each member of a tithing was accountable, financially, for the conduct of the other members. Tithing, compounded, formed into a "Shire" headed by a "Reeve," hence the evolution of "Shire-reeve" to "Sheriff."

Henry I, in 1116, divided England into districts and established a set of laws to apply to all of England. The minor crimes were divided from the more serious, and the jury system began its evolution through this period. However, the hue and cry was still the principal method of apprehending offenders.

In 1195, knights were appointed by Richard I to see that all men over the age of fifteen were loyal to him. A little more than fifty years later, these knights became known as Peace Wardens and were eventually given judicial powers. Not many years later, he appointed Coroners to each county to make inquiries into all sudden and unnatural deaths. Shortly after 1285, King Edward I established a watch and ward system for metropolitan London.

Edward III issued an act that created "Justices of the Peace" in 1361. This act again placed the function of police and the function of judge into one person. They heard all felonies, cared for prisoners, and saw that people went to church, as well as acting as the eyes and ears of the King. They had the authority of the crown and could arrest and imprison "according to the offense."

London had a police force of approximately one thousand watchmen for the night hours. In 1737, George II allowed the city to impose taxes to pay for this service. This is probably the first known use of tax money for law enforcement services.

Henry Fielding was appointed magistrate for Westminster in 1748. A few years later, he helped develop the formal organization of the Bow Street Station from which our first crime scene investigators or detectives evolved. The Police in England remained little more than a group of semiorganized untrained group of people, until approximately 1830 when Robert Peel, the Home Secretary, introduced long-needed reforms to Parliament. The reforms brought about revolutionary improvements. Peel deserves great credit for his activity toward developing a police service that earned the respect of the citizens of Britain. By 1890, a retirement plan for police officers had been developed as a probable result of earlier work by Peel.

United States

Law enforcement in the United States in 1840 was somewhat similar to the development of the law enforcement intelligence service, one hundred years later. In 1844, New York State legislated money for the development of a state police system and also provided for the development of municipal police in communities throughout the state. In the next twenty years, most of the other major cities followed. Recruitment and promotion finally became a question of qualifications rather than political patronage, though not totally.

Still unanswered is the origin of that elusive thread of history that clearly reflects the formalization of the police intelligence service. Was it Fouché in France, Peel in England, Bastillo in Italy, or just where did it begin—or has it yet begun?

Petrosino

Maybe it had its origin in New York City in the early 1900's when the "Italian Squad" was formed under the command of Joseph Petrosino, who came as close to becoming a legend in his own time as any policeman may ever (see *New York Times Magazine,* March 12, 1944).

Petrosino, born in a community near Naples, was brought to this country at the age of six. He grew up in "Little Italy" and at the age of fourteen was shining shoes on the Bowery. He eventually went to work as an inspector at the city dumps and was soon promoted to foreman. At the urging of Police Inspector Alec Williams, Petrosino joined the police force. Petrosino patrolled a beat in the West Thirties for several years and then was promoted to detective and sent to Police Headquarters.

After clearing a number of puzzling homicides, Petrosino was chosen to head the newly formed "Italian Squad." In the four years that Petrosino directed the squad, they sent over five hundred men to prison. From this, the reader, knowledgeable in intelligence affairs, may reflect that the "Italian Squad" was a special enforcement detail rather than an intelligence unit.

This is not quite true. Petrosino compiled extensive files on all questionable characters, and years after his murder it was revealed that he had gone to Italy to obtain the criminal records of men on his suspect list. He was planning to round them up and deport them. He had urged Congress to revise the immigration laws to forbid the entry of anyone with a criminal record.

In the Plaza Marina in Palermo, Sicily, there is a small bronze tablet set in the sidewalk where Petrosino was ambushed by two unknown assassins. Petrosino's death caused a sensation and, ironically, he is remembered as the man who smashed the Black Hand Society, yet proving before his death that no formal organized Black Hand Society existed; that this was a myth perpetuated by the families of the Sicilian Mafia and Camorra.

The 1920's

The twentieth century brought many problems to law enforcement in the United States. Al Capone, Baby Face Nelson, and others were to leave a scar on American Society for decades. Their machine guns, muscle, insurance, numbers, narcotics, and other evil, compelled police to become more specialized with each new modification of crime. Yet for the most part, the only intelligence activity performed was done to effect immediate arrests. Most police administrators failed to grasp that arrests rarely affect the "organization" for each underling is easily replaced.

The Boston police strike of 1919, provoked an Executive Order from President Wilson which established a precedent for police everywhere in this country. Substantially, the order prevented police from striking anywhere at anytime. The strike may have been a symptom of a far greater problem—politics, graft, and organized crime. We should observe that graft and corruption do not develop overnight. Had an effective intelligence community existed within law enforcement, it is doubtful that conditions would have reached the level they did.

After the stock market crash, during the hard years of the depression, a labor market of many more talented and honest men became available to police administrators. Still no formalization of the intelligence service occurred though some Federal agencies began to develop small specialized units for surveillance of special problems.

S. I. S. of F. B. I.

The year 1940 probably marks the beginning of a partially organized intelligence service within law enforcement. The Federal Bureau of Investigation was assigned the responsibility for intelligence gathering in Central and South America. The Special Intelligence Section (SIS) within the FBI performed many outstanding feats and played a major role in defending our nation in the critical years of World War II. The major contribution to the intelligence community was that of filling an existing void. (See *The FBI Story*, by Don Whitehead, for a thorough understanding of the magnitude of the task.)

The FBI's intelligence activities made a far greater contribution to law enforcement than is perhaps realized by many. The development of an "intelligence consciousness" among lawmen spread rapidly as a result of the impetus given by J. Edgar Hoover's training schools for intelligence activity. This may some day be credited as one of the great contributions that Hoover made to municipal law enforcement.

The formation of the "International Association of Chiefs of Police" permitted the exchange of ideas and information as well as the development of a closer personal relationship at the top administrative level. This organization, though not necessarily an intelligence agency, did permit and assist in the development of the intelligence service. Many of the Chiefs were former FBI agents with an intelligence consciousness as part of their law enforcement orientation.

Municipal Police Intelligence

After World War II ended, men returning from military service, many of whom had participated in the intelligence activities of the various branches of the armed forces, entered law enforcement. Undoubtedly many were anticipating the application of their military intelligence learning and experiences to the field of municipal law enforcement or related fields. With their return, small intelligence communities began to develop with the profession; one of the best examples of this occurred in California. Though many years of discussion, trial and error, and hard work preceded the event, it did occur; the municipal police intelligence community created a formal organization.

"On March 29, 1956, a group of law enforcement officers representing twenty-six police and sheriff departments from seven states, met in San Francisco, California. Also present were representatives of the State of California Department of Justice and the Bureau of Criminal Identification and Investigation. Those present had been personally invited to attend the meeting by the San Francisco Chief of Police, Frank Ahern and Captain James E. Hamilton, Commander of the Intelligence Division of the Los Angeles Police Department.

"The invitations had been extended to those who, if an organization was formed, should cover the widest possible area at this time and who were known to be law enforcement officers with a sincerity of purpose. There were many in law enforcement equally well qualified to attend such a meeting, but in the interest of achieving the objectives of this meeting, it was necessary to limit the attendance.

"The need for some means or organization in law enforcement to exchange confidential information of certain individuals and organizations as well as a central clearing house for this information was outlined to the group by Chief Ahern and Captain Hamilton. This was to supplement that which was already obtainable through regular police records.

"The California State Bureau of Criminal Identification and Investigation (CII) accepted the responsibility of acting as the clearing house should some organization be established and while there was much discussion among those in attendance regarding procedure, they were unanimous in their desire to form a participating group.

"Policy and operational procedures were explained and then discussed by the group. Out of this first meeting came many rules that are now the foundation for operations and membership. Among these are the following:

1. A member department must have an Intelligence Unit with at least one officer (other than the Chief of Police) responsible for its operation.

2. The information submitted to CII on forms to be adopted would be general in nature and contain only that which could be docu-

mented. Should one of the member agencies desire further knowledge of the subject, it was their responsibility to communicate directly with the agency that submitted the information to CII.
3. It is further recommended that the Membership Committee consider applicants on the basis of necessity after considering whether or not the area is sufficiently represented in the organization.

"The Operation Committee recommended the following which were also approved:

1. CII would receive the information on a standardized 5 x 8 card, make the necessary reproduction and disseminate it to the members as a routine procedure.
2. Each member department shall contribute in writing to CII such information as the Committee on Scope shall deem pertinent.
3. The dissemination of confidential information not included on the form sent to CII is the responsibility of the submitting agency as to whether he shall report it to another member.

"The Scope Committee recommended the following which was accepted by the membership:

"The purpose of this organization shall be the gathering, recording, investigation and exchanging of information concerning local or any known individuals and organizations whose background, activities or associates identify them with any of the following criminal activities:

1. Bookmaking, principals only
2. Fixers, known or suspected—Those who would be in a position to be of service to anyone included in the other groups.
3. Gambling house operators
4. Mafia
5. Narcotics, principal peddlers
6. Pimps and Procurers
7. Racket attorneys
8. Racketeers, known or suspected who do not precisely fit into one of the other groups.
9. Receivers of stolen property such as fingermen, etc.
10. Roving professional gamblers.

"This information shall extend and supplement that which is ordinarily furnished to and by CII.
"The Name Committee submitted "Law Enforcement Intelli-

gence Unit" (LEIU) and needless to say, the name was adopted. From this time forward, the Law Enforcement Intelligence Unit became a family of dedicated highly skilled professionals, constantly seeking tenacles of the "Organization."

"In annual subsequent meetings LEIU developed and refined membership requirements and general particulars regarding the operation and function of this intelligence family. They also learned the value of the personal approach to obtain valuable information essential to effective police planning and operations.

"After the passage of several years, members of LEIU found it necessary to develop subdivisions and zones in order to deal more effectively with the problems of obtaining critical data. By 1961, the direction and general management of LEIU had been allocated to an executive board consisting of five members. Membership and associate membership had been granted to agencies thoughout the United States, including large agencies on the eastern seaboard. A rule had been previously adopted to restrict membership to municipal police agencies and Sheriff departments. This rule has since been modified."

Police operational intelligence has probably made more advances in the last twenty years than it did in the previous century. Though an embryo service, the future appears exceptionally bright, full of vast unexplored areas for research and development not yet unveiled. Police agencies throughout the country are experimenting in one degree or another with the application of intelligence techniques. The product of this experiment coupled with current research in the fields of psychology, criminology, sociology, and data processing techniques should bring forth a highly effective tool for future police administrators.

This is exemplified by the current development of The National Crime Center, the development of data processing systems at the State levels, the research of criminal behavior patterns by sociologists, and the application of statistical psychology for crime prediction.

CHAPTER TWO

TYPES OF POLICE INTELLIGENCE

What to look for in this chapter . . .

The definition of intelligence;
The different forms and types of intelligence;
How intelligence relates to police administration.

INTELLIGENCE DEFINED

S ome mystery and conjecture have surrounded the functions, and perhaps even the definition of intelligence. Some police administrators believe that intelligence is a magic wand that in a single stroke will resolve all of the problems facing the agency. On the other side of the coin is the belief that intelligence is a costly luxury that few can afford.

The intelligence process, instinctive or conscious, is common to almost every level of human activity. When a man comes home three hours late, and, in response to his wife's friendly inquiry, relates that he was working late at the office, an intelligence cycle has begun. The pursuit of intelligence is the search for information required for decision or action.

There are several definitions of intelligence each having some merit. Modifying the definition found in the *Dictionary of United States Military Terms for Joint Usage,* we could say that intelligence is ". . . the product resulting from the collection, evaluation, analysis, integration, and interpretation of all available information which concerns one or more aspects of criminal activity and which is immediately or potentially significant to police planning." In 1955, the Hoover Commission in their report of Intelligence Activities defined intelligence as follows: "Intelligence deals with all the things which should be known in advance of initiating a course of action."

The aim of the police intelligence unit is to supply the chief of police or his authorized representative with complete and accurate information. If having this will not automatically produce a decision for the executive, it at least may increase the probability of the correct decision. This increase in probability may many times be the difference between success or failure.

It must always be born in mind that, in theory at least, *intelligence is not a direct action agency*, and should never be interpreted as such. The net worth of intelligence can never be evaluated by traditional thinking regarding the number of arrests performed. To evaluate intelligence using traditional methods will drastically limit its effectiveness and reduce it to little more than some specialized enforcement unit.

Within the last several decades only a very few municipal police organizations have utilized an intelligence division. Those agencies utilizing an operational intelligence unit have found that traditional police methods and thinking are not adequate to cope with organized crime and other areas requiring in depth penetration.

"What enables the wise and just sovereign to achieve things beyond the reach of ordinary men is foreknowledge," was written by a Chinese military theorist many centuries ago. Yet, for the most part, police administrators have not consistently appreciated the role of "foreknowledge" in most aspects of the police effort. They have failed to keep in mind that all divisions of society tend toward some type of organization or resemblance of the scalar principle; crime is no different.

The Typical Position

How many times has a policeman heard, "We have no vice problem, with the exception of the occasional street walker or lone phone spot." Who keeps track of this lone phone spot? For years now who has prevented him from becoming a big one? and further, is he now or will he become a member of a political complex that will cost you your good name? Certain outstanding law enforcement officers in many cities who have had to pay the price, not for what they did, but what they failed to do. They failed to keep track of what was really taking place within their community.

Captain James Hamilton, Intelligence Division, Los Angeles Police Department, in 1955, in a speech before the 62nd annual conference of the International Association of Chiefs of Police, related:

> Let's see what happens when the fish gets too big for the net. Maybe he is a small bookmaker or a policy runner who now has the money to buy what he wants. Maybe that purchase is a district attorney, a politician, or a police officer. A wise purchase—a good capital investment. Just one here and there. Then we have a shooting. The headlines say it is a territory dispute in the rackets. Or, maybe it isn't even a shooting. One or two policemen can't answer some questions satisfactorily. What happens next?
>
> The seat in the corner pocket begins to warm up. The reporters have a field day. The talk starts. The bookmakers will now quote odds on whether or not the old man will be able to ride this one out. Everyone forgets about the bank robber your men caught last week in a gun battle. The men grumble that one lousy gambler has upset the whole department. Morale drops—sometimes prices drop. More capital investments by the racketeer.
>
> Every man in this room is a realist. You have to be that or you could not have lasted long in police work. For that reason you are well aware that competent and honest police administrators are time after time caught by just such a chain of events. Given a fair and impartial hearing, they could have proven statistically that they had employed traditional police methods vigorously and resolutely. And they are right—as far as traditional police methods go. Perhaps it is time that we realists who have seen administrator after administrator fall in the same way begin to ask ourselves, "Is something lacking?" Napoleon is said to have remarked, "God is on the side with the best artillery." He was defeated by an English general who had even more faith in the efficiency of military intelligence. I would like you to consider here today the use of a formal police intelligence operating as a solution to the problem of Organized Crime.
>
> Military intelligence is not a physical attack against the enemy. Such operators must frequently pass up opportunities to strike a blow because it would imperil their primary mission—the gathering of information. The attack, the decisive encounter, is the task of offensive field forces. So it is in police work. The intelligence operator does not directly work as an enforcement officer. He cannot be judged by the number of arrests he makes, or even by the number of arrests

he makes possible. This old measuring stick is worthless when applied to an information gathering unit. Arrests cannot be assigned quantitative values. The arrest of a dozen burglars may leave the crime picture practically unchanged; the threat of arrest of an Organized Crime figure or just the fact that he knows he is under close surveillance, can completely alter the law enforcement situation.

From the viewpoint of law enforcement, intelligence can be arbitrarily divided into three major categories. These divisions should not be strictly construed for many areas of intelligence functions overlap and are not clearly separable.

Intelligence information which is primarily long range in nature with little practical immediate operational value can be classified as *strategic intelligence*. The types of intelligence activity which deal with the defending of the agency against its criminal enemies can be appropriately classified as *counterintelligence*. That type of intelligence which is of an immediate nature and necessary for more effective police planning and operations can be logically classified as *line intelligence*. (See Fig. 2.1 which illustrates the interdependence of the three types of intelligence.)

Strategic intelligence represents, more often than not, the accumulation of years of research. The maturation of strategic intelligence in most cases involves the passage of many years and thousands of man hours and many times is the by-product of line intelligence activities.

The strategic nature of this category is often implied in the fact that its contribution is difficult to assess. Who can predict the immediate value of a survey dealing with margional living in a slum section within the city? Who can say what contribution this effort will make to future police operations? The product of strategic intelligence data in many police agencies is often referred to as planning and research or in some rare cases "completed staff work." These terms, though not necessarily correctly applied, in most cases represent an intelligence product.

STRATEGIC INTELLIGENCE

All intelligence data that are not of an immediate value, in most cases, can be categorized as *strategic intelligence*. The bulk of strategic intelligence is usually descriptive in nature. The accumula-

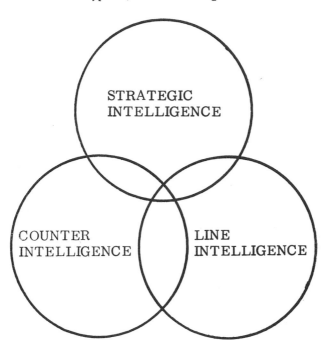

FIGURE 2.1. Types of intelligence and interrelationship.

tion of physical descriptions of personalities, who are engaged in major criminal enterprises, their vehicle descriptions, their telephone numbers, and known associates are virtually classic examples of strategic intelligence.

Further in the way of definition and by way of example, strategic intelligence is not only a by-product of line intelligence, it is many times the extra premium that is received from today's efforts. If a known criminal who may be affiliated with the "Organization" constantly frequents a flower shop and does not purchase flowers, one of several conclusions are appropriate and more reliably acceptable than others.

If a known management level hoodlum is observed on a number of occasions frequenting the company of off-duty police officers, one of several conclusions are most probable. This, however, verges on the area of counter intelligence significance. Or perhaps, it is not an intelligence activity or interest.

To simply illustrate the long-range nature of the strategic intelligence category we can elaborate on the previous example. A man has arrived home three hours late. He has advised his wife that he was working late at the office. He may receive a friendly inquiry and some terse comment regarding mealtime and the preparation of meals. If we add alcohol to the man's breath, another pertinent factor enters into the evaluation. His activity on prior occasions when he was late will undergo reevaluation by his wife. The history of the prior occasions is strategic intelligence. The alcohol on his breath is line intelligence. It is of an immediate nature and necessary for immediate planning. If we add several factors of his prior behavior, they are also strategic intelligence. Together these prior factors may equal a strategic intelligence format which will be discussed at length later.

The purchase of a bar in your city, by a known associate of a leading gangster may be of little consequence from a line intelligence standpoint, however, from a strategic intelligence standpoint, the time may arrive when the knowledge of this fact is essential to police operations and techniques. The people who frequent this bar may some day also be of consequence. The only time the knowledge of who frequents the bar can be acquired is when they are doing so. The acquisition of these data in many cases must occur by surreptitious methods. It's immediate value is subject to debate and circumstances. Its future value can run a wide range of conjecture, although, it may some day be critical.

The little street-corner bookmaker in his day-to-day travels stops at various places. Where he stops and who he talks to may be of little immediate value to police planning. Usually, this little street-corner book-maker is of no consequence to effective enforcement units. However, the names of the people whom he contacts, where he goes, and what he does with his money may be of considerable importance, yet outside the man power limitations of a vice unit. This may be appropriately classified as strategic intelligence. On some occasions it may rapidly develop into line intelligence.

The days of car bombing, various uses of molotov cocktails, machine guns chattering in the night, and similar paraphernalia used by gangsters of the past are becoming more remote. Invasion of legitimate enterprise is the new face of gangsterism. This not only creates a disarming air of respectability, it is also a means of effectively evading tax laws. It likewise creates many subtle influences which can be used to hamper overt police enforcement activities.

COUNTERINTELLIGENCE

Intelligence activity, which is concerned principally with the defending of the department against a penetration by individuals and various groups, who are inimical to the best interest and general harmony, can be classified as *counterintelligence.* It is concerned principally with the neutralizing and destroying attempts by individuals or groups that seek to discredit law enforcement. On many occasions it is difficult to separate counterintelligence activities from internal affairs areas of interest.

Most large agencies have an internal affairs division, whose main concern is the conduct of policemen and the background investigations of police candidates. A complaint by a citizen regarding an officer's immoral conduct would in most cases be handled by the internal affairs divisions, however, a complaint of an officer involved in organized crime would fall within the purview of intelligence.

Routine indiscretions by policemen should never be considered part of the foundation of intelligence predications. Probably the most serious mistake a police administrator can make, in the intelligence frame of reference, is to permit intelligence personnel to become internal investigation. This seriously jeopardizes the flow of information which is vital to the intelligence concepts. The free flow of information, from other police personnel, is an integral part of their life line. This does not mean that if intelligence personnel came upon graft or corruption or misconduct within the police department that they are to turn a deaf ear, quite the contrary! However, their future effectiveness will be dependent upon a different unit handling and developing investigations of this type.

Counter-intelligence could appropriately be involved, in a certain sense, with the origin and development of rumor and the evaluation of existing morale. Many will take sharp issue with this idea. However, in the present day it is questionable whether or not the responsibility for this important activity has been appropriately assigned to units of specific responsibility. Who within the modern police agency is responsible, "besides everyone," for the immediate destruction of malicious dividing rumors? Rumors when properly employed by groups whose purpose is contrary to the agency can virtually paralyze the efficiency of a modern police agency. This area appears to merit considerable further research by police administrators.

An internal publication of the police department, in the name of the chief of police, can be an effective counterintelligence tool. To obtain facts or material information regarding rumor, after it has undergone distillation through the supervisory line, often leads only to further confusion and rumor. The distillation, though not intentional, is in most cases conveniently classified as a "communications problem." This is many times a crutch used to lean upon to cover administrative inadequacies.

An internal publication should relate to those items which counterintelligence personnel have submitted to the chief as items of principal interest which could have a detrimental effect on field operations. This type of data should be gathered from first line personnel, not necessarily their supervisors. This publication can be produced very inexpensively and can serve to save the chief valuable planning time, though not totally freeing him from personal contact with his men. Intelligence summaries which do not effect future operations can also be published within this interdepartment resume.

In a few words counterintelligence can be summarized as *a defensive effort*, whereas in most situations line intelligence is an offensive effort. Counterintelligence can appropriately include the development of a "security consciousness" among police personnel in the handling of reports and their contents. Development of security consciousness can take many forms, such as lectures, security surveys, security inspections, and security training.

Probably the most important time to develop a security consciousness among police officers is during the days of their recruit academy indoctrination and training. A great many police recruit training academies do not include a development of a security consciousness in their personnel. Too often this is presumed or forgotten. A counterintelligence effort towards this end could very easily be integrated into recruit academy training.

In the recruit academy it would be quite easy to develop formal methods of instruction, which centered around security tasks similar to those employed by the armed forces. They appear to be applicable in all respects. The penalty for a recruit violating security by misplacing equipment, reports, and the like could be given greater emphasis coupled with the symbolizing of the consequences in actual police practice.

LINE INTELLIGENCE

Line intelligence involves both a process and an immediate product. It can be said that all intelligence is the end product of gathering and processing information. That part of the product which is of an immediate nature and essential to more effective police planning and operations can be appropriately classified as line intelligence.

From the above we can infer that line intelligence targets or objectives are many and varied. Organized crime, though a principal target, should never be considered as the only point of focus for the intelligence unit. Anything or anybody that is or reasonably could be a threat to the policies or harmony of the agency is within the intelligence scope.

As previously stated line intelligence involves both a process and an immediate product which are discussed at length in later paragraphs though briefly explored at this point. Each involves police personnel, communications, records, reports, and other staff considerations. The product of line intelligence may take the form of a daily intelligence summary, log, ledger, resume, or the like; however, many police chiefs limit this activity to a weekly, verbal or written summary, unless it is of a highly critical and volatile nature. It might be well to note that intelligence units can become a slave to a paper mill just like any other unit.

Line intelligence must *reduce the probability of error* in staff decisions. This reduction of probability of error is the principal reason for the existence of the intelligence community. Without this contribution, we have intelligence doing little other than accumulating a set of dusty files that only those cleared for confidential information can have access to.

Line intelligence can be a light that penetrates the unknown or it can be a wild scramble of misdirected or undirected, energetic speculators, each adding his own style of confusion. Line intelligence summaries, whenever possible, must be much less ambiguous than most narrative reports. Simplicity is perhaps the premium ingredient. "It is believed" or "it is our opinion" should be outlawed in almost all cases.

Line and strategic intelligence in most cases are the result of gathering information from overt sources rather than from hidden confidential informants and the like. Credit bureaus, newspapers (clipping services), transportation and communications media, plus others, form the bulk of strategic intelligence sources and the majority of line intelligence as well. However, we must concede that on many occasions, the most valuable information comes from an underworld informant. This type of highly valuable information more often than not deals with a specific crime, though on occasion it is concerned with gang operations and essential to major police planning.

Line intelligence activities involving organized crime personalities vary and the techniques of gathering information are related to many factors dependent upon the availability of money, personnel, and policies, not to mention, staff attitudes, tenor of local courts and the local or state prosecutor.

Failure to constantly observe all aspects of the black corporations will have disastrous results. The only unanswered question for failing to closely observe these people is "When will they have complete and total control of the city, the judicial process, and the police department?" It is not a question of *what* they will do, it is only *when.*

Some chiefs of police are oblivious to the symptoms of the spreading influence and danger of the "syndicate." To arrest low level vice violators has little effect on the "organization" for these pawns are easily replaced. Too often, people of the organization are stereotyped as muscle and guns, whereas we know that this is not the new image. Contributing to charities, taking an active part in the church and community youth groups, not excluding the chamber of commerce and the uptown business organizations, are all part of the disarming and powerful mask being adopted by organized crime. Police line intelligence operations that do not keep this view in the forefront are slated for the ultimate and justified wrath of the innocent victims.

Whether in search of organized crime, Communist Party activities, labor-management disputes, or nomadic hoodlums, the product will vary but the process remains relatively the same. This involves collection, processing and use of raw data, and some form of supervising or directing the collecting effort. This process is never ending and can be referred to as the "intelligence action phases." (See Fig. 2.2 which illustrates the aforementioned phases of intelligence.)

Raw information, those thousands of remote and seemingly unrelated pieces of data, become intelligence only after considerable processing. In fact, the most time-consuming and most expensive part of the intelligence action is the conversion of these raw data

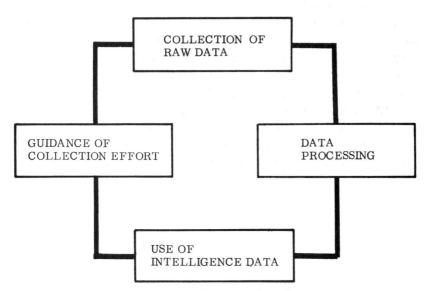

FIGURE 2.2. Intelligence action phases.

into concise expressions of activities, the knowledge of which will increase the probability of making more accurate staff decisions.

Line intelligence should always receive direction or guidance for its emphasis from the chief of police through the intelligence commander. Those issues of planning which are not completely researched and which may be of consequence to the staff in the immediate future should be of prime line intelligence importance. Failure of the chief to make these deficient areas known in advance to the intelligence commander will create serious problems; sometimes fatal mistakes will result.

A very close personal relationship between the chief and the intelligence commander will give added insurance for developing line intelligence with a high pertinence factor. A daily conference, when practicable, between these two would well serve the purpose for line intelligence guidance. This, in part, assures that the efforts of intelligence personnel are directed toward line intelligence activities with the by-product being strategic intelligence, rather than conversely.

Line intelligence is best summarized by the expression that it is the "here and now" staff requirements for more accurate decision making. Data which reach the commander of men, after he had to make a sensitive, far-reaching decision, are of little value. Data which do not contribute to present decision making are certainly not within our present category.

The patrol division has often been referred to as the "backbone" of the police department. It might be appropriate to call the intelligence division the "nerve center" that can provide a more attuned direction to the entire enforcement anatomy. When this attuning is in proper operation, the line intelligence efforts are in constant motion in a pattern consistent with staff requirements.

CHAPTER THREE

INTELLIGENCE THEORY

What to look for in this chapter . . .

What is intelligence and what is its purpose?
What are the intelligence action phases?
How are data collected, processed, and used?
What is the National Crime Information Center?
How to make your own data processing system.

M ANY misunderstandings exist in the minds of various police administrators regarding what intelligence really is. Police operational intelligence is simply the gathering and processing of information. It is not a magic formula which will resolve all the problems that may be encountered by the police administrator. Intelligence can and should do nothing more than provide the responsible authority with a better understanding of the true picture facing him. It must always be borne in mind that intelligence is not a direct action agency, and should never be interpreted as such; its net worth should not be judged by the traditional thinking of the number of arrests performed.

Purpose of Intelligence Activity

Too often administrators are required to make major decisions based upon inadequate information. Intelligence must fill the void often existing in police decision-making. Fundamentally stated, *the purpose of the intelligence unit is to increase the probability of accuracy* in operational staff decisions by gathering the appropriate information. In other terms, it can be said that intelligence is the investigative arm of the chief planners.

Intelligence Action Phases

For sake of discussion, the intelligence effort can be conveniently divided into phases which can be referred to as the intelligence action phases. The divisions are somewhat arbitrary;

however, they must include the following: (1) the *collection* of information; (2) the *processing* of the collected information; (3) the *use* of information produced from the processing component; and (4) there must be a continuous *direction* of the collection effort.

The collection effort should include a systematic exploitation of all sources of information. This exploitation must be continuous, methodical, and carefully controlled. The collection must also include a complete delivery of all of the information obtained to the processing component.

Let us look more closely at the intelligence effort (collection, processing, use and direction). Some police administrators extend the argument: "All officers within a law enforcement agency are part of an intelligence system; therefore, there is no need for a formal intelligence division." This argument is easily disputed, because the concept is ineffectual in that there is not a continuous direction of the collection effort. There is also an absence of a regimented processing instrument. Thus, the end product is totally deficient. It must always be remembered that the collection of information is dictated by the relationship of the essential elements of information that are known to the elements that are unknown. Consequently, in the "all-officers" concept, there is an unnecessary revelation of the known essential elements. A second hazard develops in the "all-officers" concept, and that is the security of the intelligence product. When security of the final product is jeopardized, the collection effort is also jeopardized. Thus security becomes the nemesis of the intelligence effort when it is applied to the aforementioned philosophy.

COLLECTION OF DATA

The collection of intelligence data is costly, time-consuming and many time its rewards or fruits will be strategic in nature (the long-range category). The great bulk of the data collected in most cases will fall within this long-range category and will thus create an unconcerned attitude on the part of some individuals. This unconcerned attitude is one of the great dangers to the intelligence effort for it is the beginning of its destruction.

It must never be forgotten that information is like any other commodity in the world. It has a value sometimes more important than gold itself. In the collection effort, a general axiom that will develop is, *"There is a direct relationship between the quality of information and the cost of obtaining it."* On occasion, this will not hold true; however, its generic application is fundamental.

The collection effort must include the development of sources of information in all levels of society within the community or police jurisdiction. It is imperative that the collection effort incorporate sources within the area of all organized crime and subversive activity. The methods and techniques are discussed at considerable length in later chapters.

The collection of information also carries with it a responsibility for its evaluation concerning reliability of the source and credibility of information. Credibility of information, though usually considered in conjunction with sources, must be evaluated whenever possible in comparison with parallel information that is already known. It might be well to state that a highly reliable source on some occasions will provide information that is not totally true. Military intelligence agencies require an evaluation of the source and information to be contained within each agent report. Below is a typical evaluation, using letters, and numbers.

Source	Information
A—Highly reliable	1—Confirmed information
B—Usually reliable	2—Probably true
C—Fairly reliable	3—Possibly true
D—Unreliable	4—Doubtfully true
E—Cannot be judged	5—Cannot be judged

By example, an evaluation such as "B-2" would indicate a "usually reliable" source and information that was "probably true."

Within the collection phase of intelligence activity, there arises that vital item, the "pertinence factor." Police operational intelligence collection efforts must contain a pertinence consideration. In other words, there must be some method to keep intelligence personnel from dashing into remote tangent areas which paralyze their total productivity with respect to the overall existing police problems. In another sense of the word, the pertinence rating is determined by the existing problems at hand.

DATA PROCESSING

The optical scanners and other refinements of the fourth generation computers will undoubtedly perform intelligence functions beyond our wildest imagination. The utilization of "single-print" fingerprint system, plus other factors, keyed to these data processing giants will rapidly identify and isolate, at a phenominal speed, members of organized crime and subversive agents. However, it is doubtful that they will ever be a substitute for the value of personal contacts by members of the intelligence community.

Though record complexes involving education, health, welfare, vehicles, driver's licenses, military service, and a thousand other unrelated specifics will be very valuable, such things as liaison programs, informant networks, clipping services, and de-briefing programs will still be required, perhaps even more than ever.

Today, as well as in the future, *the processing phase of intelligence activity is the most expensive, time-consuming activity.* The conversion of raw data into a useable product, acceptable to the vast majority, will still require the greatest expenditure of money.

Data processing involves evaluation, analysis, integration, and interpretation (see Fig. 3.1). Electronic processing of large volumes of data is new. Being "new" is a substantial part of the problem.

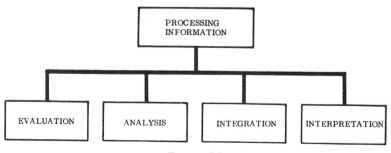

FIGURE 3.1.

It is evident even to the casual observer that law enforcement is basically not prone to try new ideas. The main problem with this philosophy is that the reluctance for most agencies to insert new techniques and methods into their operations, places them continually behind the times. Our society is moving at a pace which makes it essential that the police service become more willing to try new approaches. If a new device or technique is discovered which can be applied to the law enforcement profession, it must be given a trial to prove its worth. The *weight of tradition must be lightened.*

There are two areas in which the accumulation of knowledge will become vital in the near future. These areas are (1) organized crime and subversive activities, and (2) data processing predictions. For the purposes of this text, a complete exploration of this latter area will not be attempted. These are specialities which require specialists in their applications. The major purpose of this section will be to explore the advantages of these fields of specialization and their applications to the intelligence effort.

Acting on information from an informant, or upon speculation only, is a risk that the modern law enforcement agency many times cannot take. The basic advantage of applying statistics in the operational intelligence function is that a mathematical prediction of an occurrence can be obtained. This prediction, though many times supplementary, is essential to major planning concepts. Probability theory makes it possible to interpret statistical results. It is by means of probability theory that we can express numerically the inevitable certainties in the resulting conclusions.

The personnel of the intelligence unit will not have to become statisticians; however, they will have to learn to appreciate and have an understanding of data recovery and conversion. The main difference in obtaining data for mathematical predictions is that the data will have to be of a character which will enable a statistician to convert it into a formula. Many samples must be obtained in order to make any prediction significant. These samples of information also must be of a type which are representative of the total picture. This will influence field activity.

History of Data Processing

A brief understanding of the evolution of mathematics would be beneficial to the reader to fully appreciate the impact of data processing upon our present society. Mathematics, even in its simplest forms, played an important part in the lives of the very earliest peoples.

From the basic counting on one's fingers, or using sticks, or pieces of shells came the first big advance, the abacus. The abacus is a manual calculating device which uses beads to represent numbers. The beads are strung in rows indicating units, tens, hundreds, thousands, etc. The abacus had its origin in the Orient and is still extensively in use there today.

The first digital calculator was invented by Blaine Pascal in Paris, in 1642. The calculator he designed registered decimal values by rotating a wheel by one to nine steps, with a carry lever to operate the next higher digit wheel whenever the first wheel reached ten units.

The basic concepts in modern computing machines and data processing systems stem from the ideas of Charles Babbage, an English mathematician. In 1822, Babbage had constructed the model of a machine he called the "Difference Engine," a device which was intended to build up tables of mathematical functions from their successive differences. He had difficulty in constructing this engine; so in 1830, he conceived a vastly more ambitious project, the "Analytical Engine," a machine which could perform an assigned sequence of calculations and with the ability to store numbers, print results, and go back and cycle over any desired part of the computation. The instructions for the computation were to be given to the machine by means of a deck of punched cards, like those which determined the pattern in the Jacquard loom, a weaving machine invented fifty years earlier. It was this realization that a machine could be made to complete a sequence of calculations without human intervention which makes Babbage the originator of modern computing systems.

The history of the computer, if nothing else, demonstrates that the idea of the computer is not a radically new concept. It ıs the broadening use of the computer into fields never before considered which gives it the flair of a modern concept. In law enforcement, data processing is still in its embryonic stages; however, due to its definite advantages, it should become a standardized accepted aid within a short period of time.

Because of the computers, speed and accuracy, many people tend to consider them as almost a source of intelligence. Even though the computer can perform vast calculations almost beyond belief—this doesn't mean that computors think. They don't! Men must first acquire the raw data and then feed them to the machine. The prediction made from the data recovered from a computer is in most cases no better than the reliability and credibility of the information which was fed into it. An improper sample of data will usually result in improper conclusions or predictions.

An Introduction to IBM Punched Card Data Processing*

For almost three quarters of a century, the punched card has been utilized to solve record-keeping problems. Since the first governmental application of punched cards, their use has extended into virtually every type of commercial and scientific enterprise. The development of the cards, and the machines to process them, began as the result of a specific need. Demands from government, science and industry have brought about today's IBM punched card data processing machines and large electronic computers. They are called data processing machines because their primary function is to process business, scientific or commercial information (data) in such a fashion as to give desired results. Results may take the form of a paycheck, a commission statement, a purchase order, a customer invoice, a sales report, a profit or loss statement, or an inventory report, or perhaps a police intelligence report.

By 1885, the Census Bureau was still struggling to compile the collected facts of the 1880 census into useful and meaningful form. When it became apparent that in the future the compilation

---

* Portions of this section from IBM Publication F20-0074-0, with the permission of International Business Machines Corporation.

could take longer than the ten-year span between each census, the need was realized for a faster and more accurate way to perform the required task. By 1887, when the 1880 Census Report was finally completed, Doctor Herman Hollerith, a statistician with the Census Bureau, had worked out the basis for a mechanical system of recording, compiling and tabulating census facts. His system consisted of recording the census data crosswise on a long strip of paper. The facts were recorded by punching holes in the strip in a planned pattern so that each hole in a specific location meant a specific thing. A special machine was able to examine the holes and electrically perform the tabulation as the long strip was passed over a sensing device. For ease of handling and for durability, the paper strips soon were replaced by cards of a standard size and shape. Each card was used to record the facts about an individual or a family—a unit situation. These cards were the forerunners of today's punched cards, or "Unit records."

The IBM Card

The IBM card measures 7 3/8 inches by 3 1/4 inches and is .007 inches in thickness. The card stock is of controlled quality which must meet rigorous specifications in order to provide strength and long life. This is necessary to insure the accuracy of results, the proper operation of IBM data processing machines and the continued usability of information long after it is recorded.

The card is divided into eighty vertical areas called "columns" or "card columns." They are numbered one to eighty from the left side of the card to the right. Each column is then divided into twelve punching positions. Thus in the IBM card there are 960 punching positions altogether. The punching positions are designated from the top to the bottom of the card by 12, 11 or X, 0, 1, 2, 3, 4, 5, 6, 7, 8, and 9. The punching position for digits 0 to 9 correspond to the numbers printed on the card. The top edge of the card is known as the "12 edge" and the bottom of the card is known as the "9 edge." These designations are made because cards are fed through machines either "9 edge first" or "12 edge first." "Face up" means the printed side is facing up and "face down" means the opposite.

Each column of the card is able to accommodate a digit, a letter or a special character. Thus the card may contain up to eighty individual pieces of information. Digits are recorded by holes punched in the digit punching area of the card from 0 to 9. For example, in the card in Figure 3.2, there is a 1 punched in column 63, a 9 in column 72 and a 4 in column 77.

The top three punching positions of the card (12, 11 or X, and 0) are known as the zone punching area of the card. (It should be noted that the 0 punch may be either a zone punch or a digit punch.) In order to accommodate any of the 26 letters in one column, a combination of a zone punch and a digit punch is used. The various combinations of punches which represent the alphabet are based upon a logical structure (or code).

The first nine letters of the alphabet, A to I, are coded by the combination of a 12 punch and the digit punches 1 to 9. Letters J through R are coded by an 11 or X punch and the digits 1 through 9. S through Z, the last eight letters, are the combination of the 0 zone punch and the digit punches 2 through 9. This alphabetic coding is illustrated in Figure 3.3. The conversion of letters to and from this coding structure is done automatically by the various machines used to record or process data and it is rarely necessary to refer to data in its coded form.

The eleven special characters are recorded by one, two or three punches. Their function is to provide printed symbols as required, to cause certain machine operations to occur, or to identify various cards.

Cards are divided into segments called "fields." A field is a column or columns reserved for the punching of data of a specific nature. The field may consist of one column or eighty columns, depending upon the lenght of the particular type of information. For example, a name and address field would be longer than a telephone number field. Machine processing requires a standard arrangement of data in the card; therefore, once a field is assigned to a specific purpose, it is reserved for one kind of data in cards used in the same job.

Field length is determined by the maximum length of infor-

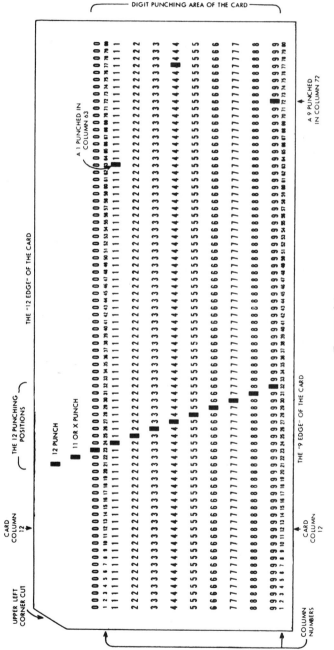

FIGURE 3.2.

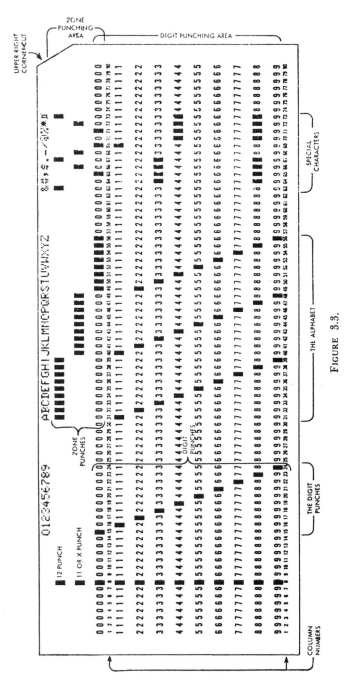

FIGURE 3.3.

mation which will be entered into the field. A numerically coded date may take up only six columns, so a field of six columns is assigned for the punching of the date. A typical date field is illustrated in Figure 3.4. A company engaging in sales activity may have only thirty-four salesmen, with no prospect of having more han ninety-nine salesmen. A two-column field would be assigned to the recording of salesman number. If the company were expanding rapidly and an increase in the sales force to one hundred or more were anticipated, a three-digit field would be assigned. Field assignment and card layout are usually made after analysis of individual needs.

Figure 3.2 and 3.3 illustrate the two most common types of corner cuts—upper left and upper right. The corner cut is used to identify visually a card type or to insure that all of the cards in a group are facing the same direction and are right side up. Card types may also be identified by the use of colored cards or the use of a colored stripe on cards of a similar nature.

Coding Data

One purpose in assigning codes to data is to enable presentation of the data in the most meaningful, orderly and useful fashion, taking into account the relationship of each item of data with other items of the same or similar nature. The ability to present related data in report form depends greatly upon the coding structure used. The assignment of codes to data is the most accurate and easiest way to express the relationship of items or information. The complexity of the relationships governs the complexity of the coding structure.

Prior to the selection of the type of code used and the assignment of the code to the data, the identity and nature of the data must be analyzed. The informational needs and desires and assignment of codes does not mean that the user must familiarize himself with the coding structure involved. Reports usually reflect the data designation by name rather than the code number, although both are often printed.

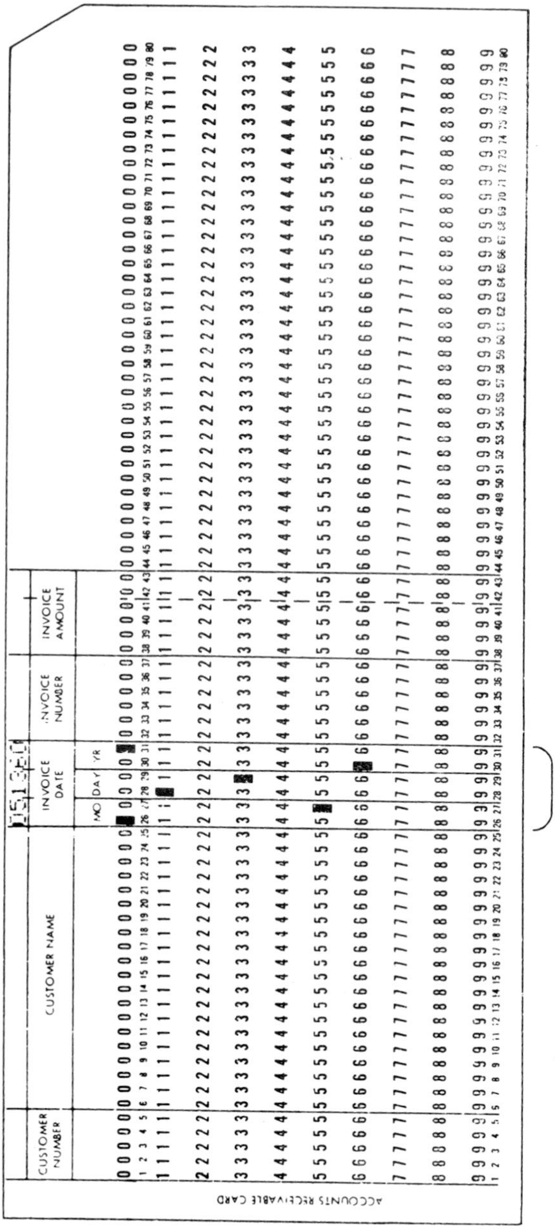
CUSTOMER NUMBER
CUSTOMER NAME
INVOICE DATE
MO DAY YR
INVOICE NUMBER
INVOICE AMOUNT
ACCOUNTS RECEIVABLE CARD

FIGURE 3.4.

Principles of IBM Machine Processing

The IBM card with data punched in it serves two major functions. The card is the means by which the data are stored; information in the card is available over long periods of time for use as needed. The card also serves as the conveyor of the data, as it is the means by which the data are introduced into IBM machines for processing.

Before data in the card are processed, the machine must change the punched hole into electrical impulses. IBM Machines operate on data which have been converted into electrical impulses. The process of converting the punched holes in a card into electrical impulses is known as "reading." Reading is done by the completion of an electrical circuit through the hole punched in a card column.

As a card passes into the machine each column goes under a separate wire brush. If there is a hole in a column, the brush makes contact with a source of electricity (the contact roller) through the hole, creating an electrical impulse which the machine is able to process. The impulse is of short duration, lasting only as long as contact is maintained through the hole by the roller and the brush. If there is no hole in a column, no circuit is completed and there is no impulse. The thickness of the card and its nonconductive qualities prevent contact. Between cards, contact is made, but no impulse is created. The principle of card reading, or converting the punched hole into an impulse, is illustrated in Figure 3.5.

The passage of the card between the brushes and the contact roller occurs at a specific time in the cycle of the machine. Because of this relationship between the card movement and the

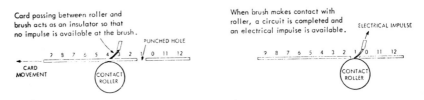

FIGURE 3.5.

machine, the difference in impulses created by different holes in a column is recognized. Thus the punched hole is actually converted into a "timed" electrical impulse. A hole in the 3 position of a column gives an impulse at a different time than a hole in the 9 position or a 4 or a 2. Furthermore, if there is more than one hole in a column, two or more impulses are created, each of which is distinct to the machine.

Once data have been converted into electrical impulses, the impulses are processed by the machine. The type of processing which the data undergo depends upon the type of machine used and the results desired. Once processing has occurred, the results are in the form of impulses also. These resulting impulses are then coverted into output form, which may be holes punched in the same card or another, a printed line, a machine function, or some combination of these.

The processing cycle is thus: cards are fed into machines which "read" the data and convert them from punched holes into electrical impulses. The impulses are processed, resulting in other impulses which are then converted into the desired output form or function.

Sorting Data

Prior to the preparation of data in report form, the data are arranged in an orderly fashion for easy use and ready reference. The process of arranging data in a sequence which will meet a specific requirement is known as sorting, or classifying. Data arrangement is accomplished on the sorter. The three basic types of classification performed on the sorter are sequencing, grouping and selecting.

Sequencing is the process of arranging data in alphabetic or numerical order, either ascending or descending. For example, it may be desirable to have a register or current transactions. Before preparing the transaction register, the cards representing the transactions are sorted on the transaction number field by means of a sorter. The transaction numbers are in ascending sequence after sorting. Thus any transaction might be referred to on the subsequent report with a minimum of effort.

Grouping is the process of arranging like items together. For example, it may be desirable to have a report showing crimes by day or date of occurrence. The cards are sorted by the date column, which results in the grouping by complete date order for the report. Grouping prepares data for reports in summarized form, or for analysis of like data.

Selecting is the process of extracting a desired time or times of data from a larger file of data. If all crimes of robbery are needed to prepare a special analytical report, it is possible to remove them from a file of all crimes. This is done on the sorter without disturbing the sequence of the remainder of the field. Because of this ability to select specific data, reports reflecting only items under consideration may be prepared.

There are a number of different IBM sorters which may be used for data arrangement. They range in speed from 450 cards per minute to 2,000 cards per minute.

An IBM sorter operates on one column of data at a time. If the data field being sorted is five digits in length, the group of cards must be sorted five times. Alphabetic information may also be sorted. Two sorts per column are required, one for the digit punch of the letter, and the other for the zone punch.

Printing

Printing is performed in two different manners. Data may be printed from cards with one line printed per card. This method is known as detail printing, or listing. Detail printing is performed when complete information is desired. All of the information in a card or specific segments of the data may be printed on the report form in the sequence desired. At the same time, amounts may be added and subtracted in counters for totals.

The other way in which data may be printed is by group printing. In this method of printing, data from cards is summarized by each different classification. The line printed for a particular classification contains group identification and the totals. Group printing is performed at speeds up to 150 per minute, or faster in later models.

The Control Panel

The machine complex is instructed to process data by means of a control panel. A few of the functions of the control panel are to tell the machine what data to print from cards, where to print it, what to accumulate and by what groups, and when to print the totals. The control panel gives the machine its flexibility, because by changing control panels a new set of instructions for processing data is given to the machine. The control panel makes possible the processing of diverse jobs in unrelated areas calling for various reports.

In each section of the panel, there are rows of holes which pass through the panel. In each hole, commonly called a hub, is a metal socket. When the control panel is inserted in the machine, each socket on the front of the panel is connected to the internal wiring of the machine. By joining two hubs with special wires, circuits are completed which cause various operations of the machine to be performed.

Some of the hubs are connected to typebars which do the printing, others are connected to counters which will accept data for addition or subtraction and still other hubs are connected to cause machine functions. As cards feed into the machine, the 80 columns are read simultaneously by separate reading brushes. Each brush in turn is connected to a hub on the control panel. In order to print the data in a card column, the impulse created in reading the column is directed to one of the typebars by connecting the hub from the reading brush with the hub connected to the typebar. The completion of this circuit causes the character in the column to be printed on the report.

The process of preparing the control panel for use is known as control panel wiring, or board wiring. Prior to any wiring, the job must be planned. The purpose of the machine complex is to process available data and put it in a form desired by management. The first step is to determine the format of the report, consistent with available data. Once the report is designed, the control panel is wired, taking into account the design of the report and the layout of the card. The sequence of data on the report does not have to conform to the sequence of data in the card.

Once the panel is wired and the cards are in sequence, the particular report is prepared by inserting the control panel in the machine, taking the few necessary setup steps, putting the cards in the feed hopper and pushing the start button. Thus the machine is able to process completely different reports with a minimum of time spent in setup, making more machine time available for processing. Control panels for regularly prepared reports are usually wired once and held for subsequent use.

The case of wiring control panels facilitates the preparation of special reports when desired by management. As needed, and dependent upon the availability of data in cards, reports may be prepared quickly to meet special or changing requirements.

Controls

Accompanying any system are safeguards to insure the accuracy of all data in the system and to insure the presence of all pertinent information. These safeguards are known as "controls." Controls are also an integral part of the successful application of IBM machines and methods. Controls not only provide accuracy of data but permit easier audit by providing a clear and concise audit trail by which transactions may be traced back from end to beginning.

Accuracy of conversion of source data to IBM punched cards is assured by verification. Next, a register is prepared on the accounting machine, a complete listing of all data punched into the cards. Then totals which accompany the source data are compared to totals on the register. The data totals are entered into the system of controls.

Accounting totals maintained throughout processing assure the accuracy and completeness of data. Comparisons of totals on reports with control figures should signify correct results. If the comparison indicates missing data, standard procedures facilitate swift referral to the original register, from which the data may be repunched and returned to the system. When normal care is taken in the handling and processing of the cards in which the data is punched, loss of data is rare. Controls are designed to assure the completeness and accuracy of reports upon which management decision is made.

A Breakthrough

With the computerization of police record systems, the time is rapidly approaching when police administrators will be able to perform intricate intelligence functions which will be measured in seconds or fractions of seconds. Predictions of far-reaching magnitude will be the result of the sophistication and application of industrial methods and techniques.

It appears that a major breakthrough is forthcoming in Dactoloscopy. The present Henry System of fingerprint classification is, for the most part, a public relations tool, generated by the news and entertainment media. Grid computerization of single prints may lead to the time when a criminal may be identified from the single print that he left at the scene of a crime.

Intelligence summaries of far reaching effect will be available to the smaller agencies. Crime and traffic accident forecasts will be prepared, within sufficient time, to permit the application of more selective techniques.

Business transactions of management level criminals will be integrated, analyzed and processed within hours rather than months. Today this is almost an impossibility, yet with current development of the National Crime Information Center, we are rapidly approaching this capability.

Data processing for a giant intelligence complex takes on proportions that are difficult to comprehend, in fact difficult to imagine. In the sections that follow, with the kind permission of J. Edgar Hoover, Director of the FBI, the authors have reproduced his basic material on the National Crime Information Center.

A NATIONAL CRIME INFORMATION CENTER

A new and powerful weapon was conceived for law and order when, in September 1965, the FBI embarked on the development of a national electronic information system to be known as the National Crime Information Center.

With rapid progress being made to place this vital network at law enforcement's disposal, the center is being set up by the FBI to complement the development of electronic information systems—metropolitan or statewide in nature—and to coordinate the setting of standards which will enable all systems to readily interchange information.

Ultimate Goal

The planners visualize an ultimate information network encompassing the entire United States which will make available to each law enforcement agency, in a matter of seconds, the facilities of an information file national in scope. No longer will the mobility of today's criminal element afford a sanctuary, even temporary, as information will be readily available to any participant in the system concerning any criminal or criminal act, regardless of geographic boundaries.

The prospect of such a system excites the imagination of the law enforcement community as it would enable local officers, through coast-to-coast and border-to-border co-operation, to close ranks against the criminal element.

Need for State-Local Systems

The logical development of electronic information systems proceeds from local metropolitan systems to statewide systems and then to a national system. In effect, each succeeding system would afford greater geographical coverage. The information stored at each level will depend on actual need, with local metropolitan systems naturally having a data base much broader than that of either the statewide or national system. By the same token, state systems will store information of statewide interest which will not be stored within a national system. It is most important to avoid any concept that a national system eliminates the need for systems of lesser geographical scope metropolitan and statewide systems must develop to serve local needs which could not possibly be met by any national system. The ultimate nationwide network will not be achieved until such systems develop in each state and the larger metropolitan population centers.

As a major step to establishing a nationwide system, the FBI has contracted with the Institute for Telecommunications Sciences and Aeronomy, Environmental Science Services Administration, Department of Commerce, to survey all existing telecommunications networks throughout the United States and to recommend a network that would best support a nationwide computerized system. It will comprehensively cover the following points:

A study of National Crime Information Center computer characteristics.

A study of existing information systems.

A study of existing and planned telecommunications networks.

Determine data transmission requirements for the National Crime Information Center system.

Develop telecommunications options to fulfill National Crime Information Center requirements.

Initially the FBI's National Crime Information Center will include stolen automobiles unrecovered after a specified time, stolen property in certain categories, and some wanted persons. The information stored in the national system will largely be entered directly into it by participants and will be immediately available to local users throughout the United States on direct inquiry. This step-by-step approach was adopted as the most practical means of establishing the nucleus of a nationwide network and of putting such a network into operation. Other applications will be added as they become feasible.

Gains in Technology

Progressive law enforcement has always been quick to recognize the value to scientific and technological advances which could improve its operations. Many tools used in the never-ending war against criminals and rising crime rates have had their origin in the research laboratory. We have seen startling developments in scientific detection methods, as well as dramatic improvements in the communications field, increase our effectiveness over the years although these have not been universally applied because of economic reasons. It would be difficult, for instance, to visualize operating an efficient police agency today without the availability of a crime laboratory or the use of radio communications facilities.

One of the more recent technological developments and one which has had, and will have even greater, impact in the field of law enforcement, is the computer. This highly versatile electronic device is currently being used to assist in police management and to provide information for operational functions. A means of storing and rapidly retrieving needed information is vital to the efficient and effective operation of any law enforcement agency. It is only second in importance to a staff of highly trained and conscientious personnel.

On the management side, the computer can compile reams of statistical information not only for standard budgetary applications but also for use in crime reports, the analysis of traffic accidents, and optimizing of manpower allocation and distribution. Further, management services possible include the compilation of necessary time records for tabulating payrolls, the recording of personnel files so that various surveys such as checks for particular talents may be rapidly conducted, and the storing of equipment inventory and maintenance control data.

On the operational side, today's computer is capable of furnishing needed information concerning crime and criminals in a matter of seconds, so that the officer on the street has a veritable wealth of information at his command at all times. A few departments are effectively using files on warrants and stolen automobiles which are stored in computers for immediate retrieval.

FBI Experience

The FBI has long been in the computer field and currently uses the computer to process over eight-hundred programed tasks. These tasks range in scope from the preparation of FBI payrolls to the analyzing of evidence in accounting cases, crime analysis, recidivism studies, and the breaking of codes. All work assigned to computers to date has necessarily been limited to that which could be processed sequentially due to constraints imposed by available equipment. However, with the developing of computers having random-access storage and the resultant adaptation to operational use through communications advances, it becomes apparent that the FBI can contribute a valuable and constructive service to all law enforcement.

Center's Heart

The high-speed computers which will make up the heart of the

National Crime Information Center will be located in FBI Headquarters in Washington, D.C. The center is expected to be in limited operation with several of the existing local systems tied into it sometime this year. This proposed network is highly complex in nature, and it may be a number of years before computerized systems at local levels are fully developed. However, this will not prevent a centralized law enforcement center within a state from using a comparatively inexpensive remote terminal which will give it full use of the services provided by the national system. Security of the information in file in the computer against unauthorized removal or access will be assured by a number of means both in the equipment itself and in the "programs" by which the equipment operates.

Information Selected

The National Center will store information selected by elements of mobility or special significance, and through communications switching, it will eventually permit each State and/or metropolitan center to exchange with each other. Other Federal investigative agencies and FBI field offices will also be in direct communication with the national system.

Standards Necessary

The initial study in connection with the National Crime Information Center showed that the several systems already in limited operation were not altogether compatible and as a result, could not effectively interchange information.

It became apparent in early planning stages that in order to have an efficient network which would ultimately give nationwide coverage, certain standards would have to be formulated. The assistance of the Committee on Uniform Crime Records, International Association of Chiefs of Police, was requested. On February 15, 1966, at a meeting in Washington, D.C., this committee resolved to establish a working advisory group to develop the necessary standards. The members of this advisory group were drawn from those departments having operating systems or those which are in the advanced stages of planning such systems.

The first meeting was held March 23 and March 24, 1966, in Washington, D.C., and represented were departments from the following cities: Boston, Massachusetts; Chicago, Illinois; Detroit, Michigan; Kansas City, Missouri; Los Angeles, California; New Orleans, Louisiana; New York City; Oakland, California; Phoenix, Arizona; St. Louis, Missouri; San Francisco, California; and Washington, D.C. Also represented were the California Highway Patrol, the Michigan State Police, the Pennsylvania State Police, the New York State Police, the Los Angeles County, California, Sheriff's Department, the California Department of Justice, the New York State Identification and Intelligence System, and the FBI.

Representatives of the Royal Canadian Mounted Police, which organization is at present engaged in a study to determine the value of electronic data processing as it applies to law enforcement in Canada, attended this meeting in an observer capacity.

While it is not necessary that any two agencies use equipment of the same manufacturer, it is necessary that messages sent between local systems or between a local system and the national system use the same coded definitions and for practical reasons use uniform formats. It is anticipated this advisory group will complete its work and furnish initial recommendations to the committee by May of this year.

Communications Advances

Paralleling the development of the computer, new communication methods have been devised so that it is now possible for a person several thousand miles away from a computerized file to interrogate that file by any one of a number of typewriter or phonelike devices and receive a response in a matter of seconds. This brings the benefits of a computerized information system within the reach of numerous police departments which, for various economic and other reasons, do not have their own computer installations.

Of course, the most important practical benefit resulting from technological advances in computer and communications design is the improvement of law enforcement performance in the prevention and control of crime. Keep in mind that the degree of effectiveness with which courts and correctional services function in the administration of criminal justice is entirely dependent upon police success in the solution of crimes. Immediate access to crime incidence and police activity data will enhance police management decisions. More dramatically and at least of equal importance, police operations benefit from the availability of "instant information." The officer on the street and the investigator as well can now make inquiry of stored police information and get a "real time," i.e., up-to-the minute, answer in a matter of seconds. Certainly, reasonable cause to detain or arrest will continue to demand rapid access to all available information.

Local Applications

As an example of current operating systems, the California Highway Patrol has experienced marked success in supplying law enforcement agencies throughout the State, and in some surrounding states, information as to whether a questioned vehicle has been reported stolen. Approximately one hundred and forty agencies are directly connected with the computer in Sacramento. An officer of any of the agencies, even while on the street, may make inquiry of the system and have the information requested in less than a minute. Similarly, agencies in California may make inquiry of the system and have the information requested in less than a minute. Similarly, agencies in California may inquire concerning wanted persons whose records are stored by the Alameda County installation. These two systems have been joined so that a single inquiry from anywhere in the State can elicit information from both computers.

In St. Louis, considerable work has been done in computerizing manpower allocation needs, as well as storing information concerning arrests and stolen autos. These systems represent the advent of a new "tool" in law enforcement records keeping.

A further application has been implemented by the New York City Police Department which is converting a sizable portion of its criminal fingerprint files to computer storage. This system, of course, requires manual classification for the storage of fingerprints and has a limited application with regard to larger files because of the conversion problem.

Interstate Cooperation

As an example of the service possible through a national system, a situation can be visualized in which a patrol car checking the parking lot of a shopping center in Washington, D.C., during the early morning hours spots a suspicious-looking automobile bearing Illinois license plates. The officer radios his dispatcher who, through the use of a remote terminal located in the dispatcher's office, queries directly the FBI's National Center. The immediate reply advised that the car in question has been reported stolen by the Chicago Police Department. This information relayed to the officer on patrol gives him information needed to immediately initiate appropriate action. Until now, many hours might have been consumed in establishing the stolen status of the vehicle or more than likely, no inquiry would have been made.

In another example, an individual arrested in a bar in New Orleans, Louisiana, on a disorderly conduct charge is taken to headquarters for booking. A remote terminal is used to check the National Center, and it is learned the arrested person is wanted in California on a charge of murder. In the past, this individual would have been held a short time and released on payment of a small fine before his wanted status became known through the exchange of fingerprints with the FBI.

Cooperation Sought

Many local and state agencies were contacted prior to the decision to proceed with the FBI's National Crime Information Center. All local and state officers consulted agreed that such a system would be a tremendous step toward more efficient law enforcement throughout the nation. They concurred it was a step which should be immediately taken before the number of non-compatible systems developed became so great that no effective network could be established. The FBI has for years, since 1924, been successfully collecting and exchanging criminal identification and other crime records with local law enforcement agencies. Now the computer, as a new tool, promises to make this cooperative effort of law enforcement more efficient and effective.

Another important area being studied by the FBI is the development of a scanning device which can be used to read and accurately classify inked finger impressions and translate such classifications for computer storage. In September 1965, proposals were solicited from more than thirty of the major companies active in this field looking toward the manufacture of a prototype. The development of such a device obviously is of prime importance to the national information network discussed, and the FBI is closely following all advances in this field. A rapid positive means of fingerprint classification and the translation of such classification into computer language will be an invaluable identification factor.

The national network described promises new horizons in effective law enforcement which could not be planned until now. It will provide the most vital information on a plane once thought impossible. This network, however, can only be as successful as the individual agencies throughout the country make it. Certain rules will have to be followed, standards adhered to, and conscientious consideration given to the principles involved. The National Crime Information Center, utilizing computerized files for information exchange, constitutes a new and powerful weapon against crime in our time, but does not alter the traditional concept of local and state autonomy in the control of crime. (See Figure 3.6 for the proposed coverage by the national network.)

POOR MAN'S DATA PROCESSING SYSTEM

The National Crime Information Center will be a revolutionary tool for law enforcement. However, by the time it becomes completely operational and immediately available to such communities as those having populations of less than fifty thousand people, a considerable number of our youthful officers will have grey hair.

In the interim, mechanical methods of data processing may be necessary to fulfill the existing void. The authors believe that there are a host of techniques in this area that are completely undeveloped. We have devised a "poor man's data processing system." It is certainly nothing new in principle, however, the application is unique.

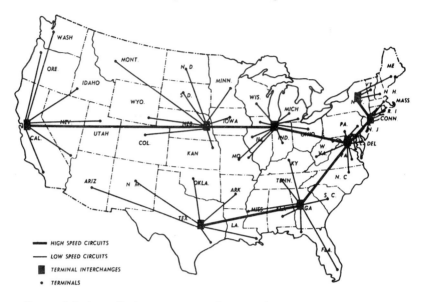

HIGH SPEED CIRCUITS
LOW SPEED CIRCUITS
TERMINAL INTERCHANGES
TERMINALS

FIGURE 3.6. A preliminary concept of a completed nationwide network.

Materials

All that is needed is approximately five thousand blank data processing cards, a rectangular sorting needle, and a V-shaped margin punch. The total cost is probably ten dollars or less. An existing shallow file drawer will serve to hold the cards.

Purpose of the System

The poor man's system can serve several purposes. One application that is easily adapted is vehicle descriptions and license numbers. A witness at a scene of a robbery may report only a sketchy description of a suspect and the color of his car. If the data were properly gathered and punched into the cards, this description could be sufficient to identify the culprit.

Gathering the Data

The gathering of the data should be based principally upon the locations within the city which are frequented by the criminal elements. For example, if you have a bar that is frequented by criminals belonging to a particular ethnic group, so much the better. Gather the license numbers and complete

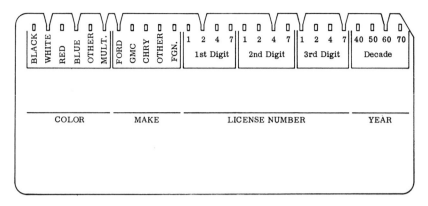

FIGURE 3.7. White and blue multicolored Ford, License digit, 248, 1960 decade.

vehicle descriptions, disregarding the registered and legal owners, of vehicles that park in the general vicinity. It makes absolutely no difference if you happen to obtain descriptions that will probably be of no consequence. You are not seeking people, only empty vehicles parked in a particular area.

The vehicle descriptions must include make (Buick, Ford, etc), color and color combinations, approximate year of the vehicle, and license number. Unusual characteristics, such as spotlights, damage, and other oddities, may be coded as an added premium.

The gathered data can be recorded initially in several different fashions. Patrol officers assigned to regular beats can be issued pre-printed data processing cards; or, they can record the data on field interrogation cards transferring it later; or, special teams using tape recorders can read license numbers and vehicle descriptions in the tape recorder as they cruise the designated areas. This information is then later punched into the margins of the cards as indicated in Figure 3.7.

GENERAL USE OF INTELLIGENCE DATA

Access to the intelligence products is one of the most important issues facing any police administrator. Few questions take precedence over, "Who should have this information?" Lack of careful consideration of this question can have disastrous consequences.

Two principles preclude the release of intelligence information. First, there must be the "need to know" on the part of the recipient. "Need to know" is not necessarily determined by a person's position in the organizational hierarchy. "Need to know" is usually akin to the task performed. Secondly, a potential recipient should be "cleared" by responsible authority as being eligible to receive the intelligence data. Line commanders, particularly those in patrol and detective functions, after proper security orientation, should be designated by the chief of police. Those designated should know each other.

Confidential sources are the lifeline of the intelligence effort. They must be protected at almost any price. Therefore, it is apparent that the "need to know" and proper clearance of the receiver are surpassed by the consideration, "Will the use of the data destroy or endanger a source of information?" One informant in the right place is worth many divisions of uniform police officers or detectives. Generally stated, operational intelligence data having a medium-to-high probability of compromising the source should not be released until it has been "sanitized" (source identifying features removed).

Staff Use of Intelligence

A weekly intelligence summary is probably the most common intelligence product available for staff use. The format for this summary will vary widely from jurisdiction to jurisdiction, however, it could include the following: In general terms a summary of organized crime activities; subversive activity that will affect general police operations; minority activity, gang activities, particularly juveniles; a concise summary of crime and traffic trends; information regarding nomadic hoodlums; and a concise statement of vice activities. The summary need not be limited to these aforementioned areas. Anything which would aid operational considerations would appropriately be included. The purpose of the summary is to inform, thereby increasing the probability of accuracy in staff decisions.

The summary should be constructed in such a nature that

preparation is easily accomplished at a particular time each week. The responsibility for the construction of the intelligence summary can be appropriately placed on the assistant intelligence commander or some other person who is concerned more with the administration of the intelligence unit than with the field intelligence operations.

Intelligence summaries should be sanitized prior to dissemination to the staff. Once dissemination is made to the staff, security problems have multiplied many times. Security measures, initiated prior to dissemination, are always more effective than those enacted later.

The informal uses of intelligence data are probably more significant than realized by many. That morning cup of coffee between the intelligence commander and the chief of police can be extremely beneficial in increasing the probability of accuracy in major discussions. This conference provides a means for the chief to acquire current data that the intelligence unit may have acquired in the preceding twenty-four hours.

CHAPTER FOUR

POLICE AND CIVILIAN RECORDS SYSTEMS

What to look for in this chapter . . .

The organizations that have major records systems;
What these organizations have available;
The necessity for liaison with these organizations.

I<small>F</small> an intelligence officer had just one reliable contact, in a few major organizations, who maintain a well-organized records systems, he would be able to obtain intelligence data of an extremely valuable nature on many organized crime or subversive figures. The purpose of this chapter is to draw attention to some of the major records systems that are available and that can be utilized if the problem is approached diplomatically by the intelligence officer.

CIVILIAN RECORDS SYSTEMS

City Directory

The City Directory is a private publication which contains full and detailed information on the entire civic, social, and industrial activities of the community. Its purpose is to direct. It is a permanent history of the community. It may be found in the public libraries, larger business establishments, chambers of commerce, local publishers or branch officers of the publisher. Back copies of the city directory enable the investigator to check over an individual's personal history: his business connections, changes of address, marital status, movements within the city, and job changes. It also enables tracing back the history of business firms or any other activity listed in the directory.

The contents of a city directory will vary from city to city. In most cases, the proper use of the city directory will provide answers to the following questions about an individual: Name? Wife's name? Telephone? Neighbors? Occupation? Does he own a business? Is he an officer in a corporation? Who are the others in the same business or profession?

Usually answers to the following questions about a business concern will be found in the city directory: What is the correct name? What is the correct address? Who are the officers? (if a corporation) What is the description of products or services? When was it established? Where are branches located?

Quite often answers to the following questions about clubs, societies, associations, etc., may be found in the city directory: What is the complete name? Where are the headquarters? Telephone number? When and where do they meet?

Credit Agencies

Commercial credit agencies contain volumes of data which if available to the investigator, would save him much time by providing him with corroborative material and leads. Some of the agencies are Dun and Bradstreet, Credit Bureau Reports, Hooper-Holmes Bureaus, O'Hanlon Reports, local or affiliated credit bureaus, National Association of Retail Credit Men, and Local Merchants' Associations.

Developing contacts within these companies and services having recorded information which might be of value to the investigator is an important part of the task. It will enable him many times to get the desired knowledge merely by telephoning, thereby saving him time and effort which are major factors in investigations.

Insurance Companies

Insurance company records systems will generally include information on all policy holders and additionally on people who have filed claims against their respective companies. Many insurance companies pool claim information to a central point in order to obtain some protection against people who continually file false claims. The applications and investigations reports on life insurance policies many times contains pertinent intelligence data regarding specific personalities. Many of the larger companies have advanced data processing methods permitting rapid access to remote fragments of information.

Telephone Companies

Every telephone company publishes a directory and strange as it may seem, most policemen do not realize the information potential in this document. Most libraries, in large cities at least, have directories for other large cities and adjacent communities. By example, and in addition to name, address, and telephone number, the yellow pages will give you names, addresses, and telephone numbers of business competitors, professional groupings, churches, and other private institutions.

A second major publication of almost all telephone companies is the Street Address Directory. It contains a listing of streets in alphabetical order or numerical order. By knowing the address, the officer can immediately determine if there is a "listed" number at the location and what it is. An unlisted number must be obtained in a different manner.

Many telephone companies also publish a Cross Reference Directory. It contains a listing of all telephone numbers in numerical order. By knowing the number, you can rapidly establish the address where the telephone is located.

One of the most important records systems in existence are those maintained by telephone companies. Their toll records and tickets normally indicate the number calling, number called, person called, person receiving the call, date, time, length of call, and on occasion transfer numbers.

The business office of most telephone companies will usually have written contracts on file with subscribers. The contracts, besides bearing signatures of the subscribers, are many times accompanied by personal history statements and other reference leads.

The telephone companies usually have a "Special Agents' Office" which investigates damage to company property, employee theft, and insurance claims of a various nature. A close liaison with the special agents' office is of mutual benefit. The intelligence officer who goes out of his way to provide maximum assistance to these special agents will be able to perform his own task with greater ease.

Also, within a typical telephone company, you can find the Wire Chief who normally has supervision over the equipment in a large central facility. The Chief Deskman, Chief Line Assigner, and Plant Service Foreman have custody and control of records regarding cable locations, terminals, and access points. These records reflect the number of telephones on the premises and any special telephone equipment plus the date of each installation and maintenance activities. For example, a small garage with twenty subscriber lines would be of intelligence interest.

Utility Companies

Utility companies (gas, lights, and water) will have records systems that will include most of the following: Name of the person subscribing at a particular address; previous addresses of the particular subscriber; amounts of the product consumed; dates of service; payment dates and amounts; and method of payment (check, money order, or cash). These records systems can be quite helpful in locating individuals or in identifying associates.

Transportation Facilities

All airlines have fairly good records systems, specifically their flight manifests or passenger listings. These will include names, flight number, date, and point of departure and destination. Crew names, along with the names of other passengers, are also available in most cases. In keeping tabs on nomadic hoodlums, the airlines are a valuable records source.

Railroads, steamships, and even taxicabs, maintain a records system, many times a very good one. Passenger lists, times, dates, and destinations are almost always available. However, taxicabs normally do not have passenger lists, but they do have "trip tickets" and driver's logs which usually show point of loading and unloading along with dates and times.

Financial Institutions

Loan companies, banks, mortgage companies, and the lending institutions contain a wealth of information. Rarely is money advanced to any individual or organization without the routine personal history statements and financial statements being filled out. These statements sometimes include the entire history of an individual and on many occasions, a number of his friends or associates are also listed. From the standpoint of intelligence inquiry, these sources cannot be overlooked. Their recent utilization of computer systems for posting money transactions makes this source even more valuable. The transfer of large amounts of capital by prominent hoodlums may be indicative of activity, the knowledge of which is vital to effective intelligence operations.

Newspaper Indexes

Most newspapers maintain a depository or morgue in conjunction with an alphabetical file indexing people and organizations with particular issues of their past editions. One of the most important safeguards against organized crime and subversive activities is an alert, honest news media. In fact, some newspaper reporters develop a side hobby or an avocation in keeping abreast of either or both. It is well for intelligence personnel to become friends with these reporters should there be any in their community.

For those police agencies which have not yet developed a clipping service or an intelligence unit, one of the first considerations after identifying particular personalities, should be the duplication of newspaper clippings from the past. With cooperation of local newspapers, this can be easily accomplished, and in most cases with little or no cost.

Service and Professional Organizations

Local medical and dental groups will have or will be able to easily obtain information on members. Each reputable doctor or dentist also keeps a fairly good record system pertaining to his patients. It can be said that virtually every hoodlum of intelligence interest has been attended by a physician at one time or another. Every intelligence dossier ought to include the name of the subject's physician, past and present.

Civic and fraternal organizations normally have a list of their numbers. They usually also have forms which include names of people who recommended any particular member. Relationships and associations of the elusive white collar criminals can be readily identified through these sources.

Merchandising Firms

Grocery and merchandising concerns of sufficient size employ what are generally termed "special agents" or investigators, not to be confused with door guards and plant security as generally understood. Many of these investigators form associations or groups and meet regularly. The records systems of these associations and their companies contain vital intelligence data. Some of their data processing methods are more modern than most police agencies. Their arrest-release records may contain intelligence data that can be found nowhere else.

Bonding Companies

Many times these agencies, in addition to a general records system containing personal history on hoodlums, will have extensive investigation reports on personalities and organizations. Most will be willing to cooperate mutually with an intelligence unit.

Private Investigative Agencies

The National Auto Theft Bureau, the National Board of Fire Underwriters, Pinkerton, Burns, Wackenhut, and many others have records systems that reach nationwide. Their intelligence capabilities should be of continuing interest to any intelligence unit within law enforcement. Mutual cooperation is discussed extensively under "liaison" in later chapters. Many times, private agencies can penetrate various groups more rapidly than law enforcement.

Public Records Systems

A vast records system exists in each of the below mentioned agencies. The intelligence officer should develop methods and contacts which will permit him to acquire information from each. The titles suggest the type of information available, though most have extensive additional data.

Automobile registration (department of motor vehicles) —information on all licensed vehicles and owners

Bureau of vital statistics—births, deaths, marriages, divorces, etc.

Census reports—spouses, children, occupations, length of residence, etc.
Courts—criminal and civil proceedings, dispositions, witnesses, attorneys
Corporations commission—owners, officers, stockholders, subsidiaries, etc.
Drivers licensing—all drivers, photos, fingerprints, and descriptions
Employment (public and private)—personal history, employment record, etc.
Health and welfare—personal history, medical, financial
Hospitals—details on all admissions and personal history
Libraries—library application forms (filled out to acquire library card)
Licensing division—business owners, professional people, others
Probation and parole—complete details on all clients
Register of deeds—land and property transactions, plus other documents
Schools—children, parents, truants, and delinquents
Tax records—all property owned and taxes paid
Voter registration—names, addresses, party affiliations, length of residence

The success or failure of the individual intelligence officer in obtaining information from the above agencies will be directly related to his personal efforts in developing acquaintances within each agency. A smooth working relationship cannot be developed overnight. It will take time, effort, and consideration. Friendly sources within these agencies are part of the life line of the intelligence effort. They must be developed.

POLICE RECORDS SYSTEMS

Every agency with police powers maintains a records system. Some are poor but for the most, we can say that they possess a valuable intelligence ingredient, principally investigation and arrest records.

Federal Agencies

At the Federal level there are virtually hundreds of subdivisions of the government which have current intelligence data of value to municipal law enforcement. To cover this completely, it would require a separate volume. Our intention is to explore those agencies that are most often likely to possess line intelligence information. The different divisions of the Department of Justice and Department of Treasury probably contain the bulk of the more valuable data. Each division possesses extensive records systems. A great part of the total effectiveness of each of these divisions can be found in their liaison programs with municipal law enforcement, particularly their intelligence arms. The records systems general subject matter for each is as follows:

FEDERAL BUREAU OF INVESTIGATION: Criminal and subversive files.

FEDERAL BUREAU OF NARCOTICS: Organized crime personalities and narcotic traffic.

BUREAU OF CUSTOMS: Importers and exporters.

ALCOHOL TAX UNIT: Distillers and brewers.

IMMIGRATION AND NATURALIZATION SERVICE: Alien registration and immigration passenger and crew lists of foreign vessels.

Others:

INTERNAL REVENUE SERVICE, INTELLIGENCE DIVISION: All criminal income tax violations.

CIVIL AERONAUTICS ADMINISTRATION: All civilian aircraft and pilots.

MARITIME COMMISSION (U.S.): Records on all personnel involved with docks, warehouses, and common carriers by water.

POST OFFICE DEPARTMENT: Tracings, mail covers, addresses of people as well as forwarding addresses.

INTERSTATE COMMERCE COMMISSION: Common carriers in interstate commerce.

DEPARTMENT OF AGRICULTURE: Listings of food canners and meat packers.

DEPARTMENT OF LABOR: Past investigations of labor racketeering.

The intelligence units within the various branches of the Federal government maintain separate records systems. Once the proper confidences and working relationships have been developed, municipal intelligence units can readily obtain nationwide data that may have an effect on local crime or subversive activities.

State Agencies

Many of the states, which have a statewide police agency, have intelligence units and records systems. Those that do not, usually have a number of organizations at the state level which perform various intelligence services. The authors, being more familiar with the State of California, cite it as an example. Within the state level in California there are at least five agencies that perform an intelligence service in one form or another.

Bureau of Criminal Identification and Investigation (CII) maintains an intelligence unit and in addition, performs a statewide intelligence service by collecting and processing crime data reported by municipal police and county sheriffs.

Department of Alcoholic Beverage Control, Intelligence Unit gathers intelligence data pertaining to alcoholic beverage and intra-state transactions of same.

Department of Agriculture, Bureau of Market Enforcement gathers information on possible violators of some of the agriculture laws and presents the information to the appropriate enforcement and prosecution agencies.

Adult Authority, Special Services Unit assists local parole officers and law enforcement by providing current line intelligence regarding prisoners-at-large who are considered more dangerous than most.

Department of Professional and Vocational Standards, Athletic Commission seeks information on gamblers and 'fixers' in the sport world.

Each state government has numerous sub-divisions. The majority have fairly good records systems. Most will assist municipal police, particularly those with intelligence units.

Municipal Police Agencies

All municipal police agencies maintain records systems though many are not adequate. Their records may range from complex computer systems down to a shoe box containing three by five cards. The same is true of their standards and proficiency. Yet, the great majority have one single thing in common: cooperation. The desire to assist other agencies may not be waning, however, the work load due to the crime rate increase and public attitude is restricting outside requests to bare essentials.

Strange as it may sound, many police officers are only vaguely familiar with what the capabilities of their own records systems are. Such basic things as crime location files, vice files, stolen object files, and monicker files are too often neglected.

Most municipal police agencies maintain a central index or reference file which directs a person to a particular case incident. In addition, these files may contain such things as field interrogations, pawn slips, ex-con registrations, and numerous other pieces of information. This central index is probably one of the most valuable tools of law enforcement, and a critical source of intelligence data.

Necessity for Liaison

Liaison programs are discussed at length in later chapters; however, it seems appropriate to mention the subject at the present time. The reason liaison must be maintained with a great many of the organizations mentioned in this chapter lies in the simple premise, "coverage." Without proper coverage, the entire intelligence product is deficient.

CHAPTER FIVE

PRINCIPAL AREAS OF INTELLIGENCE INTEREST

What to look for in this chapter . . .

The History of organized crime
The contributions of Al Capone and Lucky Luciano to organized crime
The criminal code of behavior
The symptoms of organized crime in a community
An intelligence format for the recognition of a business-crime front
An exploration of the history and theory of Communism
Unconventional warfare

ORGANIZED CRIME

Regardless of name, simply stated, organized crime is a reality; it is not a myth. Whether you call it Mafia, the Combination, the Organization, the Syndicate, or Cosa Nostra, Shakespeare's lines are quite applicable, "A rose by any other name . . ." The invisible government of crime is incomprehensible to the average American. The breadth and sphere of influence is so fantastic that it is difficult to accurately describe. It is doubtful that there is a political complex anywhere in existence in this country that cannot be influenced by one or more segments of "the syndicate."

Where did it all begin? Most authorities point to Sicily and Italy and the development of the Camorra and the Mafia as the beginning of the techniques and methods used by organized crime in this country. The historical development has some significance to the intelligence unit in that it reflects the close knit family ties of the ruling hierarchy of crime in this country. Some authorities indicate that there are approximately two dozen families that control the majority of the criminal syndicates. The family structure may be as indicated in Figure 5.1.

An Organized Crime Family

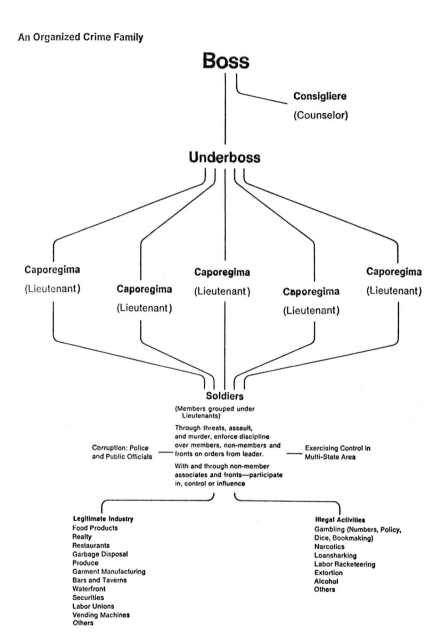

FIGURE 5.1.

A great deal of credit must be given to the Federal Bureau of Narcotics and their intelligence efforts in combatting organized crime for many of the breakthroughs are a product of their activity. Providence has also played a major role in providing intelligence data regarding organized crime. In June, 1962, in the Federal Penitentiary in Atlanta, Georgia, Vito Genovese kissed Joe Valachi on the cheek. Valachi's interpretation of this as a "kiss of death" led to a series of events which culminated in Valachi's confession regarding the inside view of organized crime in the United States. Though Valachi revealed little that was not already known, the impact was tremendous. Before Valachi, there was little public evidence to indicate anything so gigantic existed yet today.

Historically speaking, other revelations may have been just as significant as Valachi's statements. In approximately 1938, nearly twenty-five years prior to Valachi, Abe Reles, alias Kid Twist, made similar shocking revelations. Reles was one of the top agents of Murder Incorporated and was gifted with a photographic memory. During his confession to Kings County District Attorney's Office, New York, Reles recited details of approximately eighty-five Brooklyn murders of which he had personal knowledge. He also estimated that the syndicate had probably committed in excess of one thousand murders across the country. The revelations of Reles provided the base for the successful prosecution of over fifty people, eight of whom went to the electric chair. The confession of Reles left little doubt that a giant cartel of crime did in fact exist and reached across the entire nation.

Over the years, law enforcement has established that various rulers of the criminal syndicate have met at different locations in this country to plan their future activities in crime and to define jurisdictions for their operations. Of all these meetings, none carried the drama that resulted from the activities of Sgt. Edgar L. Croswell of the New York State Police. On November 14, 1957, at Joseph Barbara's hilltop mansion in the Appalachian countryside, an intelligence breakthrough of monumental importance was made known to the American public. At this meeting, more than sixty of the leading figures of crime were identified as being present; however, it took the advent of the Valachi confession and the passage of six years to remove complacency of many law enforcement officers in this country.

Probably the major achievement that accompanies the Appalachian discovery was in the fact that the American press gave it considerable play. The word Mafia and its synonyms appeared in virtually every major newspaper in this country. The resulting greater awareness did give impetus to the further development of the intelligence community within law enforcement.

Though they were not all present, such names as Joe Adonis, Albert Anastasia, Willie Moretti, Frank Costello, Charlie Fischetti, Vito Genovese, Tony Accardo, Joe Profaci, Phil Kastel, Meyer Lansky, Vince Mangano, Lil Augie Pisano, Mike Miranda, Joe Bonanno, Joe Magliocco, Tommy Lucchese, and Carlos Marcello, began to take on greater significance within the law enforcement profession. Their associations and activities began to receive a more specialized scrutiny. It gradually became more apparent that the Mafia was the matrix of the aggregate of organized crime within the United States.

Organization Efforts of Al Capone

In describing the devil in favorable terms, we could at least say that he is always busy. So with Capone—though very bad, we must concede he was an organizer of top management quality.

Capone was raised in the pool rooms and streets of Brook'yn. At an early age, he developed a strong admiration for Johnny Torrio who eventually dominated a great part of the Chicago rackets. With Torrio as his tutor and idol, Capone eventually rose to become the absolute ruler of Chicago's gangsters. Capone's organizational capacity would have undoubtedly qualified him for a top management level position in legitimate enterprise. The efforts of Capone in uniting the various criminal factions in various larger cities established a reign of criminal rule which still, in part, exists today. An example of Capone's foresight is reflected by the fact that he had numerous crews engaged in wire tapping to obtain accurate intelligence data regarding all of his adversaries.

Capone was eventually convicted and sentenced to eleven years in a Federal prison for income tax evasion. The vigilance of a Federal judge in replacing a jury that had been tampered with played a major role in Capone's conviction. The end of Capone's rule, like many before and after him, was the result of the actions of a few honest men with courage and vigilance. Such is the role of police operational intelligence.

Salvatore Lucania, The Beginning of the New Look

Salvatore Lucania alias Charles "Lucky" Luciano became the second major organizer of the Mafia in this country. In his early years he was a gangfighter, and was involved as a "mule" for a narcotics peddler. By early 1921, he had become a close associate of Giuseppe Masseria who held a staff position in the brotherhood. As Masseria rose in prominence, gaining control of the eastern bootlegging empire, so did his lieutenant, Luciano. During the prohibition era, Luciano developed two powerful friends, Joe Adonis and Albert Anastasia, the organizers and rulers of Murder Incorporated.

It is believed by several authorities that in April, 1931, Luciano participated in the murder of Masseria who was becoming old and refused to give up his position as one of the ruling "Dons." Masseria's murder provided Luciano with the opportunity to eventually become one of the undisputed rulers of the syndicate.

Like Capone, Luciano was gifted with organizational capacity. He maintained a well-dressed businessman's appearance. He demanded and enforced that everyone who worked for him do the same. This was the beginning of the new face of the Mafia, no more wide-brimmed fedoras or odd appearing overcoats. Luciano insisted that his people conduct themselves as business executives in public.

Luciano put together a prostitution organization which grossed in excess of ten million annually. He soon developed iron clad protection from Tammany Hall and eventually organized gambling, extortion, and other rackets.

The efforts of Thomas E. Dewey, *et al.*, a special prosecutor for the State of New York and a later presidential candidate, led to Luciano's conviction for the crime of compulsory prostitution, sixty-two counts. Upon conviction, Judge McCook handed him a sentence of thirty to fifty years. From prison, Luciano ultimately engineered deportation to Italy.

The intelligence activities of a Federal Bureau of Narcotics agent Charles Siragusa, who is presently the Director of the Illinois State Crime Commission, revealed that Luciano did not retire in Italy. The intelligence contribution of Siragusa is certainly worthy of high praise.

From a historical point of view, any discussion of organized crime should include the rise and fall of such people as Joe Adonis, Albert Anastasia, Vito Genovese, Anthony Carfano, Frank Costello, and many others. However, when finished with the discussion the pattern would be generally the same. The earmarks are similar, muscle or murder, extortion, gambling, political and judicial corruption, not excluding the other vices of man. Each of these men are part of families which subscribe to the general behavior pattern and code of conduct.

Code of Behavior

All of the different families of the Mafia and all of their kin folk have several things in common. Within the brotherhood, there is "omerta," loosely translated as "conspiracy of silence." However, it is more than silence; historically, it is apparent that the unwritten code of behavior for mafiosi encompasses much more. The code of behavior is probably more binding on mafiosi than the ten commandments are on present day average Christians. Centuries have gone into the culmination of this pattern; traditions to penalize violators are just as much a part of this code as any fraternal ritual of initiation, and much more effective.

Some may wonder why law enforcement has difficulty in eliminating this problem in the United States and elsewhere. When inspecting the code of behavior more closely, the reasons soon become quite obvious. They may be summarized as follows:

1. At the risk of life or fortune, or both, a mafiosi must come to the aid of a brother in need, particularly when he is in trouble with the law. This aid encompasses all things, including perjury and murder.

2. The chain of command must be respected and failure to carry out an order from the ruling hierarchy may carry the penalty of death. The ability to invoke discipline is a fact demonstrated on many occasions. This ability is unquestionably present at all times and it is performed with machine efficiency.

3. An offense against any member, by an outsider, is an offense against all members of the brotherhood. Upon command, each individual member must be prepared to avenge the transgression against the member, thus the brotherhood.

4. Appealing to the police or the courts for almost any reason is forbidden.

5. The identities of the members of the brotherhood are carefully guarded. To reveal the identities of members or admit the existence of the brotherhood is akin to treason.

6. Always have a good lawyer available or sufficient funds or methods available to obtain one.

7. Whenever possible, avoid violence against police officers, particularly Federal agents.

8. Monies given to judges, prosecutors, policemen, and politicians are investments in the future and they will bear an interest.

9. Pay taxes and invest in legitimate businesses.

Some Symptoms of Organized Crime in a Community

None of the following symptoms can be weighed singularly. Standing alone, they are of little significance. When viewed collectively, the conclusion is unmistakable. Organized crime ultimately requires the collusion of law enforcement; however, this is where a serious mistake in police estimates occur. Before collusion comes complacency and apathy or in other terms, a feeling of contentment that there is no organized crime in our community. How many times have you heard, "Organized crime cannot exist without cooperation from law enforcement and that doesn't exist here." Initially, an atmosphere of indifference is more deadly than singular bribes.

Not rating any of the symptoms in a particular order of importance, the discussion has been purposely limited to three major areas—police, courts, and businesses.

Police

Joint social participation between ranking police officers and hoodlums or shady politicians is almost a classic example or symptom that organized crime has or is about to make dangerous inroads. If this is a continuing accepted thing, then the die is probably already cast.

Police officers, particularly those assigned to vice law enforcement, living above their apparent incomes, is another indication. There is certainly nothing wrong with a new Cadillac, or a swimming pool, or a thousand shares of some mutual stock, however, financial responsibility and a policeman's salary usually prohibit these things.

Police officers with "open accounts" (receives merchandise and is not charged or billed later) in such places as bars, liquor stores, and cafes, carries a much more serious connotation than most police adminstrators like to admit. Even the continual free cup of coffee can be debated, for any journey begins with one step.

Another symptom is the broad general area of police conduct. Police officers coming up with poor memories in liquor license revocation proceedings, the loss of important evidence from the police inventory, the disappearance of police records and reports regarding hoodlums, and traffic ticket fixing are only a few that should alarm the community.

Police supervisors restricting certain types of arrests, particularly vice violations, are also indicative. When a minimum number of vice arrests are made and it is common knowledge that the community is becoming vice-ridden, then only a certain number of conclusions are available. Though not always true, one is collusion.

An unusual friendliness (hunting trips, fishing trips, island excursions, etc.) between leading defense councils and policemen lends itself to suspicion and in most cases rightly so. This takes on greater importance if the attorneys are the usual defenders of people suspected of being racketeers.

Constant transferring of police personnel assigned to various areas within the department is recommended by many police administrators. On the other side of the coin, transfers can be used to prevent enforcement activity from focusing on certain criminals and their activities. This is more specifically true when there is no formalized intelligence unit.

Courts

When a judge invokes a penalty, not consistent with his own severity index, especially when a racketeer or major vice violator is involved, then the community should take note. By example, the judge grants straight probation, after a guilty verdict by a jury, to a management level bookmaker: this may be a symptom of a much larger problem.

When witnesses constantly develop losses of memory, or too often fail to appear, or are beaten, bought, or killed, not only do you have a symptom of organized crime, you have some lazy or incompetent policemen. If this is not true, then a second conclusion is that you have a police administration that has difficulty in discerning the important responsibilities from the less important.

When the district attorney consistently declines to take criminals to court, mainly hoods with political connections, only about three conclusions are plausible. The police are not properly preparing the cases; or, there was not sufficient legal evidence, even though the police did a good job; or, because of political or criminal alliances the district attorney cannot move. When organized crime controls the district attorney's office, police are severely handicapped.

Favorable pre-sentence investigation reports sent to court from probation agencies, in contradiction to an accurate description of the defendant's behavior pattern, can have far reaching consequences and implications. The consequence of course is a breaking of the judicial chain.

Businesses

Sudden changes in ownership of long well-established firms, who are engaged in similar competitive business, may not necessarily be the result of business foresight. It may well be a monopolistic, muscle ridden, tactic of the syndicate. It may be generated by the threat to sell a similar product, at a great loss, to drive out the local competitor. Both tactics are common to organized crime. A sudden rise in the number of acts of malicious destruction of property to business which have similar products may also be a prelude to invasion by organized crime.

The presence of imported labor agitators may not necessarily be an indication of organized crime activity. However, failure to at least consider this act can have dangerous consequences, especially when it is later discovered that it was a scare tactic to enable the hoodlums to purchase the business.

When contracts are let by city government and they are awarded to the same contractors or business men over and over, the community might well be concerned. The probability for pay-off increases with each contract, and the community safeguards are lowered for this is where the shady politician is most likely to enter the picture. With· him he brings an organization. Next you have zoning variances that are totally inconsistent.

An Intelligence Format for the Recognition of a Business-Crime Front

Name and address of the firm: Present name? Past names? Addresses? Business licenses?

History of the firm: How was present ownership of the firm acquired? Was it suddenly? Where did the money come from and in what form?

Executive personnel: Who are the officers at top management level? Do these individuals have criminal records? What are the family histories of these personnel? Do they hold executive meetings at unusual hours? Do any of these personnel frequent vice locations?

Accounting: Who does the bookkeeping or auditing for this business? What is the general reputation of the bookkeeper or auditor? Who are some of the other customers of the auditor and bookkeeper?

Legal counsel: What attorneys do they retain? What is the general reputation of these attorneys? Do these attorneys have questionable clients? What law suits have they filed for this firm? Who has sued them and why? What is their bankruptcy record?

Profits: Is their declared income and overhead consistent with other firms in similar businesses? Does this business have a monitor-free cash income such as vending machines? What is their credit rating?

Raw materials: Do they fail to have problems obtaining scarce items when their competitors are having problems? What are their sources of supply? Do they export and import?

Labor: Do they employ union labor? Do they fail to have union problems when other similar companies are having them? Do union stewards or officers socialize with company executives away from the job? Any complaints of strong arm methods?

Communications: What is the pattern of their toll calls? (What firms and individuals receive telephone calls from the firm)? Do they communicate or co-operate with police during routine inquiries?

SUBVERSIVE ACTIVITIES

One of the essential elements of Communist global conquest is paralysis. Like other principles of warfare, paralysis is a condition. It is achieved by pressure. The partial or total paralysis of any agency or individual that threatens Communist global conquest is certainly a goal or a tactic of a subversive organization.

In any war, whether it be against crime or subversion or any other peoples or things, the first axiom is "know your enemy." Municipal police, more specifically intelligence personnel, will ultimately play a significant roll in the preservation of American freedom. It's quite simple, they will be some of the first to know the identities and activities of the subversive elements at the local level. In other terms, they will be the first to "know the enemy."

Dissention and public disorder arising out of induced racial conflicts are already creating some paralysis within municipal police. The creation of a general climate of opinion against 'rocking the boat' when infractions are committed by minority members is having its effect, particularly on the minds of the rookie policemen. However, before exploring present-day subversive activities, it is appropriate that we briefly examine the historical and theoretical aspects of Communism.

History and Theory of Communism

The word Communism is derived from the latin "communis" which is literally, "that which is common." In its economic sense, Communism is a society in which all things are held and shared in common. Any idiot or pseudo intellectual that thinks Communism has any relationship to the latin root word is grossly ill informed.

Communism is a pseudo-scientific, atheistic philosophy perpetrated by a criminal conspiracy of power hungry dictators. Generally speaking, in the theoretical sense, Communism has three pillars—dialectics, materialism, and economic determinism. The scientific or moral validity of each need not be debated.

Aristotle first refined reasoning or learning by argument which is the essence of dialectics. Hegel, a German philosopher, contributed the tripartite pattern, thesis, antithesis, and synthesis. In substance, the antithesis conflicts with the thesis and the result is a new level of achievement, or synthesis. Materialism or more properly, atheism, was probably taken from Feurebach who related "man is what he eats, we are matter in motion, nothing more."

In 1847, Karl Marx, a social, political, and intellectual outcast, borrowed the concepts of Hegel and Feurebach in writing the Communist Manifesto. Marx was part of the long line of history's visionary schemers seeking a magic formula for a better life without having to earn it.

His life and writings are a story of contradictions. Though the product of several generations of Jewish Rabbis, he was reared a protestant and later wrote that "religion is the opium of the people." He married the daughter of a German baron, yet later advocated the abolition of private property. Rarely did he provide for his wife and children who lived off the generosity of his friends; yet, he wrote that all people who were not of the working class were parasites.

In one sense of the word, Marx compiled a collection of economic premises which had been forwarded by many authors before him. In 1516, Sir Thomas Moore, Lord Chancellor of England, Counselor to Henry VII, in his book *Utopia* advocated "Common ownership of wealth." John Locke, in his treatise *On Civil Government,* denied the right of private property and declared that *labor is the title to property,* thus the labor theory of value.

In approximately 1650, Gerrard Winstanley wrote that war and civil strife had their origin in the private ownership of land. He viewed government as an institution of property owners and said that *religion was used to encourage the submission of the poor.* In the French Revolution, Babuef advocated *revolution,* nationalization of industry, rigid censorship, and the *giving of children to the State.* He was the first to declare that Socialism (Communism) could not be achieved without political power.

Saint-Simon advocated that all means of production should belong to a "social fund." He condemned the inherited privileges of royalty. He also was one of the first to note and describe the *class divisions in society.*

Charles Fourier advocated a society based on a "harmony of passions." There were to be no laws, no police, and no army. In addition to advocating community kitchens, he held that workers in factories should be able to change jobs every two hours.

Robert Owen professed that society should be groups of self-contained villages and that children should be taken from their parents at the age of three. He further related that each country should be one giant cooperative with a gradual *"withering away of the state".*

Pierre Proudhon *condemned private property* unless acquired by labor only. He envisioned a great national bank operated by the state in which interest and profit would gradually be eliminated.

Louis Blanc was the first to appeal to the workers for political control. He advocated state workshops for all industry to eliminate competition from private enterprise. He related that . . . *each should produce according to his ability and each should receive according to his needs.*

When looking at the contributions of the previously mentioned authors, it is apparent that the communist manifesto is a summary of material that arose out of the conditions centering around the industrial revolution of Europe. The plight of the workers during this time is certainly not comparable to modern day conditions.

There is no question in the minds of all well-informed people that communism is dedicated, by idiology and practice, to the complete domination of the world. *Communism aims to destroy all other social orders.* Communism will continue to try to advance its cause regardless of the price in human lives and suffering.

Excerpts from the writings of Lenin contribute to a great part of the strategy of world communism, a knowledge of which is necessary to completely understand what is coming. Some of the things that Lenin said would happen are . . . *First we will take Eastern Europe, then the masses of Asia. Then we will surround America, the last citadel of capitalism. We shall not have to attack. She will fall into our lap like an over ripe fruit.* Lenin also related, "The enemy may defeat us a thousand times, but the thousand and first time we shall win." Further insight to Communist philosophy is provided by, "We shall agree only so long as agreement shall strengthen us, then we shall disagree." Also, respect for law is contained in the basic tenant of Lenin, "We must be prepared to use any means, legal or illegal."

The fallacy of Communist theory and idiology can be summarized rather briefly as follows: their tripartite application of thesis, antithesis, and synthesis to the history of man fails to take into account a multitude of factors, *particularly morality, laws, religions, politics, plus many others.* Law is not an instrument of the ruling class, nor is religion. The Bible applies to rich and poor alike as do the teachings of all religions.

The history of man is not the history of class struggle. Class antagonisms have continued to decrease. There is a greater distribution of wealth under capitalism than there has been under any other form of economics in the history of man. The retrogression of man has always been the result of *moral decay*, not economics.

Dialectical materialism is as fallacious as economic determinism. Most people know that man can not live by bread alone; he is a social, political, and religious being.

The Soviets started their world conquest over forty-five years ago when they first sent agents of subversion and espionage to all corners of the world. Their assassinations reflect their determination as well as their madness.

Terror and Murder

The vast majority of law enforcement personnel in the United States believe that the Mafia is one of the most sinister forces haunting American communities. This is perhaps only partly true. A far greater enemy, the Communist intelligence systems, have claimed a great number of lives and will continue to claim many more in the future. The Mafia wants a free piece of the pie, the Communists want the whole pie.

In 1918, Felix Dzerzhinsky, the first chief of the Soviet Secret Police, proclaimed, "We stand for organized terror and this should be frankly admitted." The entire history of mankind has never seen a more vicious group of human beings than the small group of professional killers who started their march of madness when they captured the modern "Kerenski Movement" in Russia.

Lenin, the Soviet's first dictator, who has falsely been depicted as an "intellectual idealist" was little more than a murdering butcher. His troops of terrorists murdered the entire Czarist family, including their doctor, their cooks, their maids, and their waiters. These people were herded into the cellar and then shot and their bodies were hacked into pieces and soaked in sulfuric acid and benzene, and then burned. Their ashes were then scattered into a swamp. These so-called intellectual idealists during Lenin's time murdered at least several million people. Adolph Hitler was a piker compared to this clan.

Stalin, who was the heir of Lenin, in 1931 and 1932, murdered ten million kulaks and sent many more millions to the Siberian slave labor camps. In 1951, the American Federation of Labor compiled statistics, based on affidavits from 14,000 individuals, which revealed the names and locations of one hundred and seventy-five of the slave labor camps in Russia. The report also revealed that the Communists within these camps murdered almost two million people each year.

In January, 1953, Stalin launched the doctor's purge, charging that nine top Soviet doctors had confessed to having murdered various Russian military leaders. Stalin also charged his intelligence services with criminal laxity. The "medical murders" were not foreign to the Soviet Intelligence System. This particular method of assassination has more than a passing familiarity to the Soviet scheme of murder and assassination.

When Khrushchev took over control of the Soviet system, he did not do so without blood on his hands. He was no different than Stalin or Lenin. Khrushchev probably murdered as many or more people. The techniques and methods were little different.

When looking closely at the Communist scheme, we find that the murders have not been limited to those locations exclusively behind the iron curtain. They have committed thousands of assassinations in virtually every country in the world including the United States of America.

A favorite technique used by the Soviet Intelligence System for assassination is to employ medical men for the actual killing. This permits the deaths to be described in terms of natural illness. This first came to light in approximately 1938, during the Moscow purge trials. The term "medical sabotage" was officially used by the Soviet government. The Russian press proclaimed that Soviet doctors had caused the death of Maxim Gorky.

In 1953, as previously mentioned, Stalin, after receiving information from a woman doctor, had a great number of other doctors arrested declaring that they were deliberately giving him the wrong treatment. The significance of these events and others reflects some inference that the Communists are well acquainted with the use of physicians as instruments of assassination.

Virtually every country in the world can document numerous assassinations conducted by the Soviet intelligence apparatus. France, Italy, Germany, and the United States, not to mention others, have extensive documentation of murders committed within their countries by the Communist conspiracy. Whittaker Chambers, a former director of part of the Soviet intelligence system in the United States, has related that an old Communist party saying is, *"Any fool can commit a murder, but it takes an artist to commit a good natural death."* Municipal police must never forget this.

Probably one of the first Soviet assassinations in the United States occurred in 1934. Valentine Markin who at that time was head of the Soviet spy system in the United States became involved in a conflict with his Moscow superiors. He was murdered on a New York City street.

Juliet Poyntz, a native of Nebraska, and one of the leading founders of the Communist Party in the United States, was lured into a New York Central Park on June 5, 1937. She was forced into a car by two Soviet agents and strangled.

In New York City, Carlo Tresca, an editor of an Italian-language newspaper, and an avowed anti-communist, was murdered on January 9, 1943. Gunther Reinhardt, a Soviet Agent, later complained of the price they had to pay for this assassination. This assassination was probably performed by members of Murder Incorporated, one manifestation of the Mafia.

General Walter Kirvitsky, a defector of considerable importance who had previously warned a friend, "If I ever am found in circumstances which indicate that I took my own life, don't believe it." In February, 1941, Kirvitsky was found in a hotel room in Washington, D.C. with his brains blown out. A .38 caliber automatic lay on the bed beside him. Police termed the death a suicide. Many people believe that Kirvitsky did not take his own life in view of the fact that he was scheduled to give important testimony regarding Soviet espionage in this country.

Lewis Adamic, a Slav immigrant, who became a famous writer, had a long record as a tool of the Communist criminal conspiracy. He broke with Russia during the supposed rift between

Tito and Stalin and began to vigorously support Tito. Adamic's body was found in a lounge chair in his farmhouse in Milford, New Jersey, in early September, 1951. He was found with a rifle laying on his lap and a bullet hole in his head, indicating suicide. His house had been systematically set afire. The walls of the house had been lined with oil-soaked rags, a technique taught in the Lenin Academy.

Alger Hiss, a personal advisor of President Roosevelt, present at the highest conferences with Stalin and Churchill, was exposed as top level Soviet intelligence agent. There are at least five instances of unusual deaths in connection with the Alger Hiss case. It may be mere coincidence, but of those connected in one way or another with Hiss, five were to meet untimely, unusual deaths. The first was that of General Walter Kirvitsky who has been previously discussed. Just as Kirvitsky was about to unmask a top-level espionage ring in the U.S. State Department, he committed suicide.

The second strange death with a link to the Hiss Case was that of Harry Dexter White, who was Assistant Secretary of the Treasury. White was probably the most important Soviet Secret Agent in the United States Government, that is, next to Alger Hiss. Incidentally, White and Hiss along with Molotov drafted the United Nations Charter.

White only appeared once before the House Committee on Un-American Activities and discussed nothing of value. White was a very nervous person and was deathly afraid that he had been discovered. (This was established by the testimony of Whitaker Chambers.) Before the House Committee or agents of the FBI could further interrogate him, he died of a "coronary heart attack."

On October 20, 1948, the body of W. Marvin Smith, a Justice Department lawyer, was found at the bottom of a stairwell in the Justice Department Building. He apparently fell from the fifth floor where he worked. Smith was the only living person who could establish important evidence to prove Hiss' perjury or treason. What other damage Smith could have done to the Communist conspiracy is unknown.

On December 20, 1948, Lawrence Duggan, a former Chief

of the Latin-American Division of the State Department and also a close friend of Alger Hiss fell sixteen floors to his death from his office in Manhattan. New York police deemed it an accident or suicide. Insurance companies, after considerable investigation, concluded that it was not suicide and paid off his widow. Whitaker Chambers has confirmed that Duggan was a Soviet agent and could have revealed extremely damaging information regarding Alger Hiss. Hade Massing, a former Soviet spy ring courier, wrote that she had recruited Duggan to work as a Soviet spy in the State Department and then had turned him over to yet another Soviet agent.

Despite the efforts of numerous powerful allies, Hiss was eventually convicted of perjury and sentenced to prison for five years. The trial or the preparation for the trial was delayed, permitting Hiss to escape other charges. While in prison, Hiss ran into an old acquaintance, William Remington. Remington was in prison for perjury centering around his giving secret government documents to a Soviet courier. A few days before Hiss was to depart from prison, Remington was brutally murdered by another convict who bashed his head in. Little information regarding this was ever released to the public.

Raymond Kaplan, a Voice of America radio engineer was struck and killed by a truck on March 4, 1953 in Cambridge, Massachusetts. This was shortly after Kaplan had agreed to testify before Senator Joe McCarthy's Committee regarding subversion. His testimony would have centered around reasons or circumstances involving site locations for Voice of America radio towers and Communist infiltration into Voice of America.

John C. Montgomery, a State Department employee, who handled secret material dealing with Finnish-Russian Relations, died of strangulation June 24, 1953. Montgomery's nude body was found sprawled on a second floor landing with a bath robe cord and hemp rope knotted around his neck. The torn ends of the cord were tied to a third floor landing. It was labeled a suicide.

Abraham H. Feller, a former State Department official was also killed in a fall from his window of a twelve floor Manhattan apartment in November 1952, shortly after the Senate Internal

Security Sub-committee began investigating secret American Communists holding important jobs in the United Nations. This was also called a suicide.

In 1957, William E. Sherwood, who had been head of Communist discussion groups in the late 1930's, was scheduled to testify before the House Committee of Un-American Activities. Forty-eight hours before he was to testify the second time, Sherwood was found dead as a result of poisoning.

Dr. Jean Tatlock was found drowned in her bathtub on January 6, 1944. With only a few inches of water in the bathtub, the police labeled it as suicide by drowning. Tatlock, an admitted Communist, was the mistress of J. Robert Oppenheimer who was later declared a "security risk" by the U. S. Atomic Energy Commission. Other people connected with the Oppenheimer Case died at rather timely moments.

Probably one of the most unusual deaths that have occurred involving key figures of extreme importance in the anti-communist battle, was that of James Forrestal, the First Secretary of Defense. Though most Americans are not aware of it, James Forrestal was probably the most active and most influential anti-communist of his time. Virtually single-handedly, he prevented the Communist takeover of Italy.

James Forrestal was confined to a Naval Hospital and was held incommunicado for several weeks (not even being permitted to talk with his priest). Shortly before the time he was to be released, as a result of a Writ obtained by his brother, his body was found at the base of a ledge which was sixteen stories below the room that he was registered in. An analysis of the death of James Forrestal has been prepared by Cornell Simpson and published by Western Islands Publishers. It should be required reading for every law enforcement officer, particularly those assigned to intelligence activities. After one has read this revealing study, he cannot help but believe that municipal police in their short-sightedness to develop an effective intelligence community, are failing in their duty to the American people.

We could name several hundred people who have died at critical moments; in a better sense, we mean at the moment just before they were about to expose the extent and nature of

Communist intelligence operations in sensitive positions in this country. No doubt the various intelligence functions of the FBI, Army, Navy, and Air Force could list thousands.

The fantastic part of it all is that the majority of the murders are investigated routinely by local police who rarely have perceptions regarding motives which are broad enough to encompass the Soviet murder motive. Murder will continue to be a Soviet intelligence technique. Local police must always anticipate this, particularly, in deaths of questionable nature involving people who have access to our nation's secrets.

Unconventional Warfare

In February 1946, in Moscow, Joseph Stalin, in his discussions of the forces of the "new warfare," made very plain some of the things to anticipate in describing the role of the Communist Party Member and the sympathizer. He related, "The only difference between them is that some belong to the party, others do not. But that is a formal difference. The important thing is that both are furthering the same common cause."

The term "cold war," is a dangerous amorphism. As long as we blindly accept and use enemy semantics and trick labels like "cold war," "peace," "peaceful co-existence," "extremists," and "neutralism," we are furthering our jeopardy. The ultimate objective of this type of warfare is the destruction of the will to resist in advance of perceptible hostilities. General James A. Van Fleet once stated, . . . *Soviet Russia intends to build one world of Communist states through a world-wide program of unconventional warefare.*

Part of this unconventional warfare will include at least the partial or the complete paralysis of municipal police. Recent riots in major cities throughout this country cannot effectively be described as the spontaneous uprising of the oppressed Negro race.

Disruptive activities on the campuses of our finest universities and colleges are not simply products of youth gone astray. The identification of covert organization activities on the campuses plus the nature of the publications can lead an objective viewer to only one conclusion. This is simply an example of the unconventional warfare directed against the American way of life.

The development of some of the labor-management conflicts and agitations cannot be explained away as natural growth and development. Too often, effects of typical Communist Party cliches and techniques are apparent.

And still another area comes to mind, and that is the decisions of the Supreme Court of the United States. The Communists can never destroy this union of states as long as we have fifty state governments which first must be destroyed. However, through the adoption of the pre-emption theory, the Supreme Court is slowly stripping state sovereignty and protection. It appears that members of the United States Supreme Court are not aware of the nature and techniques of Communist warfare. Any other assumption would carry the implication of conscious treason by the court.

The municipal police intelligence community can and must identify and on occasion effectively neutralize the efforts of these engaged in the unconventional warfare against the American communities and nation. The data that they will provide to direct action agencies will be of the highest value. The price of liberty is much more than eternal vigilance. The Communists summarize it well, "peace is merely war in another form."

The authors suggest the reading of Raymond M. Momboisses' text *Blueprint of Revolution* for a greater understanding of the objectives and practices of the Communist conspiracy.

CHAPTER SIX

POLICE INTELLIGENCE OPERATIONS

What to look for in this chapter . . .

Identification activities of intelligence operations;
Liaison programs, with whom for what?
Clipping services, what and how;
How to recruit and develop informants;
Surveillance and its different forms;
Scope of intelligence operations.

T HE Los Angeles Police Department is more than equal to their reputation of having the finest intelligence unit in the nation. The scope of their operations is included at the end of this chapter. Any police agency seeking detailed information concerning their operations and administrative procedures will be greeted with a spirit of cooperation. The citizens of Los Angeles can be proud of this dedicated professional group whose most notable accomplishments include keeping Los Angeles relatively free of organized crime.

Police intelligence operations involve a number of different tasks, namely discovery and identification activity, surveillance, liaison programs, informant recruitment, clipping services, debriefings, and other miscellaneous activities. These different tasks are part of the actions that go into the preparation of the total intelligence product.

The miscellaneous activities may vary with such factors as staff attitudes, personnel available, funds, and the field situation. Our approach to police operational intelligence concerns itself principally with the larger departments in the metropolitan areas. However, the practices and field activity will have a general application to all intelligence units.

IDENTIFICATION

Individuals

The identification and surveillance of individuals involved in organized crime and subversive activities consumes a considerable part of the police operational intelligence field activities. The identification of the associates and relatives of organized crime personalities is vital to the final intelligence product. It is oftentimes the answer to the question "who owns who" in the community. A considerable amount of time is also spent in the identification of minority leaders, transient agitators, and local leaders. The identification and surveillance of nomadic hoodlums is also important.

Organizations

The identification of organizations, alien to the police purposes as established by law and recent custom, is a necessary activity of an intelligence unit. The origin and development of these organizations, coupled with the identification of the officers and their attitudes, is as important as their stated or implied purposes. Militant organizations which can disrupt the community or destroy lives and property, need to be covered by alert police management. Subversive organizations, particularly those that advocate the violent overthrow of the Government, need to be identified and kept under surveillance.

Locations

Locations where prominent gangland personalities frequent, need to be identified. The majority of most prominent hoodlums frequent a limited number of locations. The identification of their residences and businesses are also important to police intelligence operations. The identification of their neighbors may also be consistent with effective field operations.

Vehicles

Early identification of vehicles used by hoodlums, subversives or union racketeers is vital. In our highly mobile society, rarely is a crime committed without the use of a vehicle in some phase of the crime. Many police intelligence agencies maintain a current vehicle file with methods of rapid search based upon this premise.

Telephone Numbers

The identification of numbers belonging to anyone within the intelligence scope of operations is important. Each time a telephone number is acquired, many agencies will enter it into a separate file usually indexing it by the last three or four digits. Some agencies alphabetize and cross index their telephone number file.

Informants

A complete division of this text is devoted to the discussion of informant recruitment and development. Probably one of the most important aspects of the identification and discovery activities of police intelligence operations is the identification of potential informants. More specifically, it is vital that field operations identify personalities that may have a high probability for recruitment.

Liaison

In General

Probably the main reason more people do not actively assist the police lies in the simple fact that the police fail to personally solicit their help. Liaison is little more than making friends who have access to an intelligence item, particularly people within organizations and records systems. A liaison program is one of the principle activities of police intelligence operations. A limited liaison program will usually produce a limited intelligence product.

Specific Assignments

One of the essential ingredients of a successful liaison program is the specific assignment of personnel to specific targets. With the full realization that staff requests are usually in a constant state of change, consistent with the field situation, liasion assignments will also be subject to some change. However, generally speaking, it is necessary to have a constant liaison program, involving specific assignments of personnel, with the following enterprises: credit agencies, utility companies, police agencies of all types, the press, labor unions, and telephone companies.

A second ingredient of an effective liaison program is the reporting requirements. All teams conducting liaison should be required to make daily, reports regarding the acquisition of intelligence data. The formalized reporting requirement is absolutely essential, however, the methods and approaches may differ.

A liaison program is dependent upon several features. Assuming that competent personnel have been assigned to the unit, then we can forego this point. Competent personnel still require funds and policy guidelines regarding the use of funds in liaison assignments. A cup of coffee, or a lunch or dinner can, many times open doors and files that could never be opened otherwise. The development of effective liaison cannot fail to take this into account.

Press Liaison

Any police agency that fails to remember that the press always has the last word is slated for trouble. An alert news media can be one of the most powerful forces in a community in fighting the activities of organized crime. Liaison with the press is therefore essential.

Within most major metropolitan newspapers you may find some reporters who are more than journalists. Some have an avocation which includes the study and investigation of organized crime. Bill Farr, a reporter with the Santa Ana Register—a six figure daily publication—is such a person. Farr probably has more knowledge and insight into organized crime in Orange County, California, than 99 percent of the full-time Orange County law enforcement officers.

Active liaison with the members of the press also has a secondary operational intelligence value, beyond access to a morgue of past publications, in that they are capable of creating considerable cybernetic damage to the hoodlum hierarchy. Public implications that one or more members of the gangster crowd may be cooperating with law enforcement creates a volatile situation which causes them to make mistakes.

Clipping and De-briefing

Clipping Services

Clipping articles from newspapers in accordance with an existing format is an important method of gathering intelligence data. The communications network of modern newspapers make this an excellent source of highly valuable material.

The recovery of this data permits several options. You can do it with your own personnel either sworn or unsworn, or both; or, you can have an outside contracting agency do it for you. There may be some publications which sworn personnel within the intelligence unit will handle. Some publications may be delegated to clerical personnel. The publications within the target area of certain intelligence teams may be clipped by that particular team.

The first question that arises is what publications should be clipped (removing articles of intelligence interest for processing). In large metropolitan centers, all newspapers within the concerned agency's jurisdiction are essential. Newspapers in adjacent jurisdictions may also be important.

The next question that arises is what are the guidelines to be used, or what format is to be followed in clipping material from the newspapers. In large communities, some intelligence agencies establish a list of organizations and personalities which have, or may have in the future, intelligence significance. This format may include personalities within the respective areas of intelligence interest such as organized crime, subversive activities, labor disputes or tensions and other data peculiar to the locality.

If the clipping service is partially performed by an independent contracting agency then the format may be considerably different because of security reasons. It is obvious that the format in outside hands would be a vulnerable point when changes were made in its structure.

Some major police agencies may have clipping services that cover the major metropolitan newspapers from coast to coast. The format for clipping from these publications that are not within the immediate locale may be limited by the sheer weight of volume. In some cases, the format for these external newspapers may be limited simply to any article bearing the name of the city of the jurisdiction concerned, and only when it involves crime or subversion.

De-briefing Activities

In World War II, pilots returning from bombing missions over enemy targets were asked a multitude of questions pertaining to their observations and experiences. These de-briefings often made major contributions to the intelligence estimates and operational planning. The same principle appears to be applicable to law enforcement actions.

How many times have you heard a Chief of Police lament that he is not receiving the necessary information from his men. Patrol and traffic divisions, whose personnel constantly patrol the streets of a city, many times observe occurrences or things which they do not reduce to a formal report.

A de-briefing process must have at least two essential features. First, personnel cannot be chastised for failing to take the necessary steps at the time they made a particular observation. Secondly, there can be no embarrassment or penalty attached for failing to obtain complete details during the field experience. An example of this is as follows: Officer Jones, while having a cup of coffee in the local coffee shop, observes a prominent hoodlum drive by in a new car that he just purchased. All the officer saw was that it was a green Dodge. He failed to get the license number. In most cases, the officer would not make a formal report of this, however, its immediate and future value may be considerable.

A de-briefing program can be established by simply setting up a tape recorder with speaker where officers going off duty can have access to it. The ground rules for its use may vary. Or, an intelligence analyst with a format in mind may conduct one or two minute interviews with personnel going off duty at a centralized location. Multiply this activity by each precinct and the usable product may be surprising, particularly after an orientation period has past.

INFORMANT RECRUITING AND DEVELOPMENT

It is an exception to the general rule when the ability of an investigator exceeds the quality and quantity of sources of information he possesses. Rarely, if ever, has there been an investigator of any proficiency that did not possess many and varied sources of information. Informant recruitment and development ranks very high in mandatory achievements of an intelligence officer. Failure in this area will usually restrict the individual officer to the ranks of mediocrity.

Intelligence must use informants for several principal reasons, both in overt and covert operations. The essential coverage of various criminal and subversive elements is impossible without covert penetration. Apprehension of particular criminals and the repression or restriction of their activities is also an important aspect of information direction, control, and use. There are definite types of information that can be acquired by no other manner than through the use of informants. The total effectiveness of an intelligence unit can be fairly accurately evaluated at any given time by assessing the number and quality of informants that can be brought to bear in an instant case.

Informant Defined

The term "informant" has many connotations. To the traditional American mind, it is somewhat repulsive. From the standpoint of police intelligence operations, the term informant can be defined as "any person who provides information." With this definition, it is easy to see that it can include everybody. It is a synonymous term for source. Yet, the term more often than not connotes secrecy and clandestine affairs.

From an operational intelligence standpoint and for discussion purposes, the general term informant can be further delineated as follows: A person who casually imparts information to an officer with no intention of providing subsequent information could be referred to as an "incidental informant"; a person who is selected, cultivated and developed into a continuous source of information regarding police targets can appropriately be termed a "recruited informant."

The incidental informant may be anonymous and may impart

the information for many different reasons. The recruited informant is of particular consequence to police intelligence operations. There are several different categories of recruited informants.

Some people, by the very nature of their position in society, have certain legal, moral, and ethical responsibilities to report information to law enforcement agencies. By example, such people as school teachers, probation officers, doctors, police officers, and firemen, are included. Promptness and proper channeling of data makes intelligence recruitment in this area necessary and feasible. This category might be appropriately referred to as "spontaneous" or "automatic" informants.

Secondly, there is a broad category of recruited informants that are not under social compulsion to report information to the police. They might be referred to as the "ordinary run-of-the-mill" sources of information that are developed by an intelligence officer in his travels. They are people who, through repeated association, will provide information of intelligence interest.

Thirdly, there is a category of informants who are of a specific operational nature. Their principal direction and control is focused on the penetration of various criminal or subversive in-groups. (This should not be confused with the undercover police officer.) This group of informants is referred to by some agencies as "special employees."

Informant Motives

Regardless of the type of recruited informant involved, the fundamental motives of each individual may vary greatly. The motives may include such things as civic responsibility, material or personal gain, and a wide variety of psychological innovations. These can include vengeance, fear, revenge, jealousy, and the like categories.

Generally stated, a person motivated purely out of civic responsibility or patriotism is the most reliable; *however, he is by far the rarest.* In most cases, those individuals motivated purely out of civic responsibility have very limited access to valuable intelligence information.

One of the most common motives of recruited informants centers around material or personal gain. This gain may take the form of money, property, immunity, or protection from enemies. Still another area of motives may be related to such things as family revenge, vengeance, detective complex (discussed later) or political or professional manipulation of competitors.

It is not uncommon for rival hoodlum elements to provide information to the police which will destroy their competitors. It is particularly desirable for an intelligence unit to develop an alternating reaction in this situation.

The most common of all the psychological motives used by most nonintelligence police personnel in dealing with and controlling informants is fear. Fear, when sufficiently magnified, is a productive implement; however, the day will eventually occur when the "hammer-over-the-head" will lose its meaning. It must be pointed out that fear, though many times highly productive, must later be converted into some other emotional tool.

It cannot be emphasized strongly enough or often enough that of all things available to the intelligence officer perhaps none is more desirable and more favorable than plain, simple friendship. A genuine friendship based upon some degree of mutual respect will produce a far greater and more available product than all other things. This doesn't imply that the intelligence officer should become a "bosom buddy" with every source of information that he develops.

Informant Recruitment

The importance that can be attached to the selection of an informant might be comparable to the selection of a policeman with certain general exceptions. Broadly speaking, the recruitment of an informant involves at least four arbitrary phases, i.e., selection, investigation, approach and persuasion, and finally a testing phase.

The selection or identification of a potential informant must take into account may factors, the principal one being access to information of an intelligence nature. It is particularly desirable to be able to identify and recruit an informant who has access to many criminal in-groups or subversive organizations. This multiple access is the premium that must be constantly sought. Wide access is probably the single most important feature in the consideration of recruiting the potential informant.

All creatures, including man, can be categorized with respect

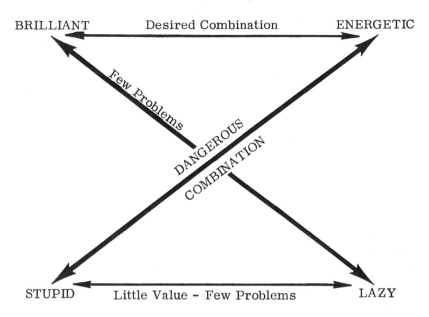

FIGURE 6.1. Informant qualities.

to basic intelligence and initiative. They range from brilliant to stupid and from energetic to lazy. With four factors involved, it is readily apparent that numerous combinations of varying degrees of intelligence and initiative exist. It is a cardinal rule that informant recruitment should meticulously avoid the combination of energetic and stupid. These are the nightmares that must be avoided at all times (refer to Fig. 6.1).

In selection of the informant, consideration must also be given to health, age, sex, education and personality. Failure to consider an informants health and age versus probable task can lead to unfavorable results and vast expenditures of manpower; likewise, personality, character, and education come into operation.

The investigation of the potential informant that has been tentatively identified as a "probable" must be as thorough as possible. The investigation must establish possible existing motives as to why this person might assist the police intelligence community. Failure to do so will deny the officer who must perform the approach and persuasion phase with little more than a guess. The investigation should not be a cursory one. It must include such things as employment, in-group loyalties, idiosyncrasies of personality, behavior oddities, plus all personal descriptive data.

After careful identification and selection of the potential informant and after a meticulously thorough background investigation which involved the expenditure of great numbers of man hours and dollars, comes the approach-persuasion phase. On many occasions, all previous efforts will hinge on a single few moments, even though the approach may and should be prefaced by numerous prior associations of an informal nature.

Because of the critical nature of the approach phase, careful precautions should be taken to create those circumstances which are most favorable to a receptive state of mind on the part of the potential informant. Such a setting might include pleasant surroundings, perhaps a confidential apartment, completely free of any aire of probability of compromise, preferably in an adjacent city or a remote area foreign to the informant's living pattern. Such props as music, lighting, interior decorating, food and proper refreshments are not to be overlooked. Every precaution that is commensurate with reasonable expenditure of funds should be taken to insure an atmosphere that will be conducive to an affirmative response.

However, in most cases, the recruitment of the ordinary informant is a gradual evolutionary process based on informal follow-up contacts by the officer. Too often this is the sole recruitment formula used. Only when the informant recruitment effort is formalized will penetration at a higher level be achievable. The formalization of the program and the pin-pointing of the responsibility is one of the essential tenets of police intelligence administration.

If the individual has been properly approached, in a formalized program, and consent has been amiable, this does not mean that the investigation of the informant is over nor that we are to neglect the very important testing phase. Future contacts with the informant will undoubtedly elicit background material that should be included in the informant dossier. Initial testing of the informant should involve some assignments to objectives, *the answers to which are already known.*

The testing program should begin, of course, with limited assignments, with a gradual integration into the more important areas. The occasional testing of an informant should continue through the entire affiliation.

Methods of Contacting Informants

Many policemen become careless in their methods of contacting informants. Too often major efforts have been paralyzed because the police officer became slipshod in his selection of a place to meet an informant.

The selection of a clandestine meeting place, on each occasion, should be made by the controlling officer, *not* by the informant. The locations and times should vary with due consideration to the officer's and informant's normal routine.

There may be occasions where it is necessary to never contact an informant directly in person. This obviously calls for the use of mail or telephone, or maybe even telegraph. It may also call for guarded or unguarded "letter drops" (message left at previously designated location, without officer or informant being present at the same time). In major operations, involving cases of considerable importance, it may be desirable to establish such things as business fronts, confidential apartments and other cover implements.

Security of the Informant

One of the most important aspects of security for the typical criminal informant is to prepare him with a cover story in the event he is observed in the company of police officers. This cover story should be simple and easily acceptable to the hoodlum mind.

The officer certainly has a responsibility for the safety of any informant who is helping law enforcement. If an officer fails in this responsibility with one informant, the word seems to pass very quickly on the street, thus hampering recruitment efforts.

Case decisions of the various higher courts may give rise to security measures that will be unusual to say the least. It is fundamental that the protection of the informant is better assured when his identity is known only to a very limited number of people. We hesitate to guess what would happen if control officers were permitted to learn only code names of informants and never true names.

Payment of the Informant

Correct payment of an informant is many times an integral part of his security. Overpayment to a low level informant can be as serious a mistake as underpayment to a high level penetration informant.

The essential features involved in the payment of an informant are not difficult. Though quality and quantity of the information produced appear to be the main considerations, another more important factor is evident. *Risk* is the essential feature, of course not totally neglecting effort. An informant who produces a small quantity of highly valuable information that was obtainable only through great risk is entitled to considerable compensation, perhaps more so than the informant who produces a high quantity of information with no risk. Reliability, of course, is not forgotten.

With some exceptions, payments to informants for information provided, is best done on a "C.O.D." basis. Most other methods are difficult to justify. It also has a tendency to improve the quality of the information. In other terms, you pay after confirmation of the information provided, with limited exceptions.

The type and amount of payment may be governed by department policy. It is imperative that each officer assigned to the Intelligence Unit clearly understands the payment policies. Payment of informants within the intelligence operations lends itself to private financing, e.g., private groups, crime commissions, etc.

It is particularly desirable to be able to obtain information without having to pay anything for it. Some agencies adopt dangerous blanket policies of never paying for information. This is unrealistic and many times outright foolishness. On the other side of the coin, informants must never be left with the impression that the officer has an unlimited bankroll. Generally stated, operational penetration informants are the type that are most likely to receive regular payments for their services.

Evaluation of the Informant

It is probably most accurately stated that the reliability of an informant hinges mainly on performance over an extended period of time. A dangerous pitfall for intelligence officers is the fact that they develop a tendency to evaluate information in conjunction with the reliability of the informant, rather than in conjunction with known confirmed data.

Informant Records

Probably one of the most sensitive aspects of vice and intelligence operations is the administrative requirement that officers reveal their sources of information. Most agencies soon adopt policies that informant records are controlled only by the Chief of Police or, in larger departments, by administrative units commanders only. Even this is not completely satisfactory to many personnel. Security of the informant record should include a separation of identity and data. The informant's true name should never appear in files which give his personal history and performance. Code name or symbol is sufficient. An informant record card or dossier should include the date of first contact and the circumstances, a complete description, prior and present control officers, criminal and political history, habits, hobbies, idiosyncrasies, a resume of cases worked on, types, amount, dates and methods of payment and an up to date evaluation of the informants reliability.

General Treatment of Informants

As in every other form of human endeavor, there are certain general rules we can apply which have proven to be effective through experience. As each informant is different, so must our treatment of him be different. Some salient points to be considered might include:

1. Avoid the use of derogatory terms in referring to informants of any type.

2. Avoid disclosing the identity of the informant which will in most cases ruin his potential.

3. Protect the interests of the informant, remember an investigator is usually just as good as his sources of information.

4. Consider all information from known or unknown informants as valuable until proven otherwise.

5. Be noncommital on the value of the information received.

6. Express appreciation for all information received regardless of its values.

7. Keep appointments on time even though the informant may not.

8. Don't get over anxious; be patient. Take your time.

9. Especially in the case of the incidental informant ask those six reliable questions deftly: Who? What? When? Where? How? Why?

10. Investigate all leads. The fact that a previous tip was of no value after investigation should not cause the investigator to discount subsequent tips.

11. Especially in the case of women informants, get all of the information the first time. Also take steps to protect yourself from false claims.

12. Keep control of the investigation. Some informants will try, intentionally or not, to take charge of the investigation. Some informants will develop a detective complex. This can be used to an advantage some of the time, other times it is a detriment.

13. Keep what you know to yourself, don't become an informant's informant.

J. Edgar Hoover once said "The confidential informant has become an institution and is used as a means of establishing truth. The use of the confidential informant is as old as man. In fact the first recorded use of the confidential informant is found in the Old Testament. As an institution, the confidential informant is used not only by law enforcement, but in practically every walk of life, particularly by the press and our financial institutions. In recent years, there has been a determined campaign designed to deprive law enforcement of the use of the time-tested and valued confidential informant. This campaign of vituperation is part and parcel of Communist strategy to convert the courtroom into a forum to discredit the judicial processes. For the most part, the technique of the smear has been devised by Communist lawyers, skilled in concealing foul and despicable acts behind the Fifth Amendment. They employ tactics which even the most unscrupulous under-world 'mouth-piece' would frown upon as improper."

SURVEILLANCE

Surveillance is simply one method of investigation. Many times it is very costly and time-consuming. Yet, the fact remains, on many occasions, there is no other manner available to acquire the needed information. The legal rules governing police surveillance will differ from jurisdiction to jurisdiction. Our approach to this type of investigation will depart from the opinions of many authors, particularly in the area of technical surveillance (the use of clandestine devices).

It is readily apparent that a brief explanation of some of the terms to be used is essential. Surveillance is observation to some; to others it connotes more than just sight. It may imply the sensory experience to many. The person doing the observing is generally termed the "surveillant" and the person being observed is usually referred to as the "subject." In some areas of the country different slang terms are used to define these and other people and things.

For discussion purposes, we can conveniently divide surveillance into several major areas. Basic principles of surveillance, covert and overt surveillance, intermittent surveillance, special techniques of surveillance, and technical surveillance are a few that come to mind. Such things as communications, security, and personnel will be integrated into the previous areas.

Regardless of the type of surveillance, whether it pertains to an individual or a location, certain concepts are fundamental to all. Yet in the same breath, it must be remembered that surveillance can produce rapidly changing situations which require the application of the best of imaginations. Few mistakes can be permitted as the stakes are many times quite high.

Reiterating, surveillance is the observation of individuals, vehicles, or locations of interest. During the process of the surveillance, all pertinent information should be observed and recorded. For an individual, the surveillance should produce the following: Who the suspect is contacting; what his activities are; of what consequence they are to the intelligence interest; where his contacts are made, and when he is making them. For an establishment or building, it may be to furnish information of the following: Who is visiting or doing business at the premises; what transactions are being carried out inside the building; when these transactions are made; and how it affects the total investigation. The main concerns for a vehicle surveillance are who it belongs to, where it is being driven, when it is used, for what it is used and who uses it.

The ability to conduct a successful surveillance is a talent that is produced by a knowledge of the various techniques, and the wisdom and maturity of judgment in their use. Some of the basic "nuts and bolts" of this task will be noted on the following pages. The ability to use the various techniques is something that will only be gained through the trial and error practice. In the covert application of surveillance, it must be noted that failure to remain unnoticed is a twofold cost. The first cost to the investigation is that hours of manpower have been lost forever. The second loss is that the suspect, once having "burned" one tail will be more alert than ever. The added caution may result in the inability for another officer to conduct a surveillance on the subject. The suspect will probably also cancel his activities thus resulting in a loss of information.

In intelligence work the surveillance is of critical importance. The suspect is not the usual run-of-the-mill criminal. Many of the individuals of interest to the intelligence unit have been "tailed" by some of the best in almost every major city in the United States. This type of individual may even have developed a second sense that he is being followed. The more suspicious or alert an individual is, the more difficult he is to follow. There are some precautions to take that will assist the surveillant from being "burned" or "made" by the suspect.

Basic surveillance

To begin with, the surveillant should be an *average type* of individual. A six-foot seven-inch individual will naturally attract attention due to his size. Obesity, especially if it is quite noticeable, of the individual will also limit his ability to remain unnoticed.

The officer's manner of dress should be such that it is conservative to the point where he is not obvious.

This also would apply for the wearing of jewelry which may be considered flashy or different. All in all, the officer to be assigned to a surveillance should be of a type that no one would pay attention to, or give special notice to.

The officer while on the surveillance should not use any disguises or theatrical gimmicks to attempt to change his appearance. *The more unusual he makes himself, the more readily he will become noticed by the suspect.* However, the changing of appearance by putting on a pair of glasses, or hat, or using a reversible coat, is, of course, more than permissible. It is the extreme changes to unusual features that must be avoided. His actions should be of a usual type for the average man. Again, conservatism is the keynote. A bouncy, active type of activity is as noticeable as the sly, slinking type. Somewhere between the race track tout type of actions and that of the super spy lies the successful mannerisms needed.

Any objects that are to be carried should be of the type that are common to the area that the officer is in. If he is in a business district where the majority of men are carrying briefcases, then it may be advisable for him to carry one also. If the surveillant is following a working man carrying a lunch bag, it may be advisable to finish his image of a worker also by carrying his own lunch bag. The general idea here is that the officer should take on the character of the area. If the majority of people within the area are carrying some type of object, it may be best to play the part and also carry a similar object. If there is no area distinction, it is best not to carry anything that may make the officer's presence noticeable.

The surveillant should always be prepared to defend his reason for being in the area. It may become necessary to explain his presence at any time. Many gimmicks can be used, from the sales pitch on down. In the selection of officers for surveillance details, a supervisor should definitely choose an officer who can think on his feet, and not be the type that will freeze on the spot if he becomes challenged during the assignment.

Eye contact with the suspect is generally considered taboo by most experienced authorities in the area. If a suspect has eye contact with the surveillant, it is easier for him to recall the officer if or when he observes him at a later date. If eye contact can be avoided, it should be. If, on the other hand, it becomes more obvious if eye contact is not made, then a casual glance is in order. An example of this may be a situation where a suspect has turned a corner, and just as the surveillant also turns the corner, he is met practically face to face with the subject who has decided to retrace his steps. Any obvious attempt to look away or conceal his features will definitely "burn" the officer.

Friendships with the patrol or traffic division personnel must take second place when a surveillance is being conducted. It is therefore obvious that a surveillant does not show any signs of recognition when a fellow uniformed officer is in the immediate area of the suspect and the surveillant. If the uniformed officer shows any sign of recognition, it is best to first casually convince the officer that he has made a mistake. The second step would be to quickly obtain a relief officer to take over the surveillance.

There are a few basic rules that should be followed when it becomes necessary for the officer to park his vehicle and remain in an area for an extended period of time. When the vehicle is being parked, the officer should first be careful to select a legal parking spot. When he parks the vehicle he should do it in a normal manner to avoid being noticed. Any actions involved in leaving or re-entering the area of the vehicle should also be done in a normal manner. If too long a period of time is spent in one spot, the suspect or someone connected with the suspect may note this detail and become suspicious. Periodically moving the vehicle is advisable. Being relieved by another unit after a period of time is even more desirable. If the surveillant must stay inside his vehicle, he should sit on the passenger side. The reason for this being if the person is seated on the passenger side of the front seat, he is obviously waiting for the driver of the vehicle to return. If he sits on the driver's side for a period of time, he will become suspicious to the residents of the area. The use of police radio or telephone calls should be held to a minimum at all times.

The basic problem with unmarked police units has always been that they are almost as easy to identify as the marked units. The predominant number of undercover units are the basic models of the Plymouth, Ford or Chevrolet. They are usually four-door vehicles with a solid neutral color. A break from this pattern will make identification more difficult. Color combinations instead of a solid color are advisable. Also the addition of accessories and a few extra chrome parts will help.

Because of the vehicle's frequent use, even the aforementioned precautions will only deter detection for a short period of time. The best method, if it can be arranged, is a short-term *loan agreement* with a local used car dealer. This type of arrangement will make possible the use of a range of vehicles from a Cadillac to a Volkswagon. As soon as the vehicle in present use becomes "known" it is merely traded for another type of vehicle.

Moving-vehicle surveillances are becoming more and more difficult to perform. Increasing amounts of vehicular traffic on the roadways and traffic signals, increases the possibility of losing the vehicle being followed. People are more accustomed to looking into a car's rearview mirror than they are to looking over their shoulder. In a moving vehicular surveillance, it is therefore important that more than one vehicle be utilized in the surveillance. The most difficult maneuver will be in the transfer of one surveillant unit to another. Here is where communications is most vital. In both vehicular and foot surveillances, the factor of communications cannot be overlooked or underestimated.

Overt Surveillance

Most surveillances are of the covert type, as previously discussed. As the reader can note, the covert type of surveillance is an unnoticed method of following or observing individuals, vehicles or buildings. The overt surveillance is naturally just the opposite type of operation. The overt type is therefore an open surveillance in which it is beneficial or at least planned that the suspect know that he is being followed. A question may come into the reader's mind as to the advantage or at least the reason why this type of method would be used.

The first advantage may be that if a suspect is exceptionally nervous he will be prone to making errors if he is certain that he is being "tailed," and that any moment he may be openly arrested. He definitely will not directly commit a crime while knowing that he is under open observation. He may, however, in a state of confusion, make contact with someone of interest to the intelligence division. Under normal conditions he may not have made the contact, but, in a state of desperation he could turn to his "boss" or "contact" for assistance, or advice. The combination of the fact that he is basically nervous, and the fact that he knows that he is being watched can yield unexpected treasures of information.

The second reason for the use of this type of surveillance is to deter the possible criminal. The type of actions conducted by the intelligence unit in this case is not the movie version. In the Hollywood production a harassment type surveillance is earmarked by physical and psychological abuses of the suspect. Nothing this crude is the basis for the overt type of intelligence surveillance under discussion here. For our use the element of harassment could not be further from the fact. The intelligence type of overt surveillance is basically to let the suspect know that he cannot perform in the particular location of city he is in at present because he will never be alone.

This type of surveillance is of course *not* wasted on a petty thief or other minor criminals. The patrol and investigation divisions can handle this type of individual without taking man hours from the intelligence division. The type of suspect that this method of surveillance is extremely applicable to is the suspect that orders the crimes, but, does not take an active part in them. If his contacts are eliminated due to the fact that he feels insecure, a major victory has been accomplished for the present time. The intelligence division for the particular locality has performed a service as the "big fish" will migrate to safer waters where maybe the police are not quite as alert.

Intermittent Surveillance

An intermittent surveillance may be of the covert or overt type. Usually though, this method is used only with the covert approach. This method is simply observing the subject a little bit each day. By example, suppose you want to locate places where the subject meets people of intelligence interest and they are not within the priority level of technical surveillance. Adding the fact that the subject is quite cautious, brings intermittent surveillance into consideration. Such is the case of a typical book-making runner (one who accepts bets or pays bettors). Each day you can follow him on a particular leg of his journey until all stops are identified.

Intermittent surveillance is a prime consideration in Intelligence Units that are under staffed. However, in conducting a thorough surveillance of a subject, *there are few effective substitutes for an abundance of experienced personnel.* Intermittent surveillance has a secondary value of some importance in that it permits more security introductions with greater ease, e.g. one vehicle today, different ones tomorrow, etc.

Presurveillance Conferences

One of the most important aspects of any surveillance that is most often overlooked or given only surface attention is the pre-surveillance conference. Most pre-surveillance conferences should consider the following:

1. The pre-surveillance conference must include the appointment of the surveillance leader or commander and his assistant. The responsibility and commensurate authority for the success of task is thus pinpointed.

2. Attendance at the pre-surveillance conference should be mandatory and all personnel involved should be encouraged to participate in the planning of the project.

3. The pre-surveillance conference should set forth the principal goals to be achieved and the general alternatives available in the event some type of an emergency develops.

4. This conference should include the presence of several additional personnel that could be assigned in the event the unexpected should arise.

5. The conference, when possible, should be conducted sufficiently ahead of time so that an atmosphere of haste does not predominate.
6. Equipment such as vehicles, radios, and special devices must be assigned to specific personnel for preparation and field testing prior to the actual surveillance. As a general rule, special devices require specialists in testing and application.
7. A telephone number must be designated, preferably a private number within the Intelligence Unit facilities, which can be used by personnel in the surveillance to receive instructions or additional information. The surveillance team leader must designate who is going to man this telephone.
8. The pre-surveillance conference must set forth a detailed description of the subject, as well as a resume of the subject's habits, haunts, and quirks. When possible, it is well to provide each surveillant with a photograph of the subject.
9. The conference should include general instructions regarding wearing apparel of the officers, with emphasis on "blending with the area" where they are most likely to be working.
10. The conference must also include considerations such as meals for officers, replacements, and the fulfilling of various requests during the time the surveillance is in progress.

Some considerations for the individual officer:

1. Every officer in almost any investigation should have a sufficient amount of small change in his possession in order that he can quickly make use of a pay telephone, bus fares, turnstiles, etc.
2. He should keep changing climatic conditions in mind when departing for surveillance assignments. Nothing is more miserable than to have inadequate clothing. This can also become a security breech.
3. Each officer should have a cover story in his mind to help conceal his presence in the event of an unexpected confrontation. The cover story should be simple and easily believed.
4. In personnel who lack experience, there is a tendency to believe that they have been discovered ("burned or made") by the subject. If the individual officer lacks field experience in surveillance, it is incumbent upon him to seek assignments with experienced officers.
5. Generally stated, it is better to lose the subject than to alert him that he is being tailed. However, this will depend upon the type of case and overall purposes.
6. The surveillant should be prepared to face such problems as a subject taking a taxi, boarding a bus or train, entering a large building, restaurant, theater, hotel, or other structure. *There is no substitute for the ability to improvise.* Imagination plays a definite

role. The basic concept is to stay as close to the subject as can be done safely. Being too close will "burn" and too far away will cause you to lose the subject.

Technical Surveillance

Technical surveillance, electronic surveillance, wire tapping, bugging, call it what you like. It is legal in some jurisdictions and illegal in others. It is employed by some and not by others. *One thing is certain, those police agencies that use it are in a much better position to protect the citizens of their respective communities.*

There is a lot of fantasy or fiction surrounding technical surveillance. If a modern police agency had some of the equipment that is conjured in the minds of television writers, they would soon win the war against crime, or at least win more of the battles. However, space-age technology may soon make some of these James Bond devices available. How soon is anybody's guess.

Within the police intelligence frame of reference, there are a few cardinal rules that should never be violated. Technical surveillance should never be employed without the cognizant authority of the intelligence unit commander. Its use should be restricted to targets that have a high probability of a good return rather than random selection of doubtfuls.

There is absolutely no room for amateurs in technical surveillance; technical sensitive work requires experienced technicians. It appears desirable that technical surveillance should be limited to a single team of specialists within the intelligence unit which can service other teams.

Clandestine devices come in a variety of forms, shapes, and sizes. Each may be used for a particular application, though many have multiple applications. Generally speaking, they can be divided or classified according to the type of target they are used against, e.g. structures, vehicles, and telephones.

A not too recent raid on a bookmaking establishment in a large metropolitan city revealed that organized crime is using these devices. Upon entering the premises the officers found no one present, only a "cheese box" (an electronic relay system to receive and relay incoming bets on the telephone). While searching the remainder of the location and discussing the case, they discovered a sub-miniature *active* radio transmitter. The results of this case need no explanation.

The shotgun microphone, parabolic reflector, and the famous cocktail-olive transmitter are nice conversational pieces for those who are so inclined to discuss this subject matter. However, from an intelligence standpoint, their value is more fiction than fact. What police need is a multiple purpose, economic device with a very low maintenance factor.

Any discussion on how to bug a telephone, vehicle, or room would be defeating. Below are two dozen firms that manufacture surveillance equipment. Most the firms will provide detailed instructions and specifications of their equipment upon request of any law enforcement agency.

George Cake Co.
621 Garvey Ave.
Monterey Park, Calif.

Consolidate Acoustics
1302 Washington Street
Hoboken, New Jersey

Criminal Research Products
Conshohocken, Pennsylvania

Dee Company
Box 7263
Houston, Texas 77008

Ekkotronics Company
P.O. Box 5334
Milwaukee, Wisconsin

Kel Corporation
778 Pleasant Street
Belmont, Massachusetts

Miles Wireless Intercom, Ltd.
598 Broadway
New York, New York 10012

R & S Research, Inc.
2049 Richmond Avenue
Houston, Texas 77006

Saber Laboratories, Inc.
1150 Bryant Street
San Francisco, California 94103

Silmar Electronics, Inc.
3476 N.W. 7th Street
Miami, Florida 33125

Steckler Sales Company
42 East 23rd Street
New York, New York 10010

Tri-Tron of Dallas
330 Casa Linda Plaza
Dallas, Texas

R. B. Clifton
11500 N. W. 7th Avenue
Miami, Florida

Continental Telephone
Supply Company
17 West 46th Street
New York, New York 10036

Dectron Industries
13901 Saticoy Street
Van Nuys, California

Dehart Electronics
P.O. Box 5232
Sarasota, Florida

Fargo Company
1162 Bryant Street
San Francisco, California

Martel Electronics Sales, Inc.
2356 South Cotner Avenue
Los Angeles, California 90064

Mosler Research Products, Inc.
9 South Street
Danbury, Connecticut 06813

S.A.C. Electronics
4818 West Jefferson Boulevard
Los Angeles 18, California

Security Electronics
11 East 43rd Street
New York, New York 10017

Bernard B. Spindel
Ludingtonville Road
Holmes, New York 12531

Telephone Dynamics Corporation
1333 Newbridge Road
North Bellmore, New York

W.J.S. Electronics
737 Seward Street
Hollywood, California 90038

Undercover Surveillance

On rare occasions it may be necessary for undercover intelligence personnel to join certain organizations for the purpose of close surveillance. Often it is possible to have these agents work to positions of leadership within these organizations; however, in most cases it is not feasible. Short-term undercover surveillance is usually sufficient. Figure 6.2 illustrates short term undercover surveillance. The arrow indicates a policeman in an undercover role observing and gathering data regarding an organization that was potentially disruptive to the community.

FIGURE 6.2.

INTELLIGENCE IMAGE

One of the secret strengths of the intelligence unit lies not in what the unit can do but rather what the hoodlums believe it can do. The fostering of this image is essential in certain quarters of the hoodlums activities. Strange as it may seem, lip service and rumor play a major role.

It is not uncommon for a hoodlum to wonder how the intelligence unit knew he was engaged in a certain illegal activity or planning such activity. Many times the intelligence unit does not or did not know; however, upon confrontation, the intelligence officer may only have smiled and remained silent. This knowing silence and smile may have given rise to fantastic rumors in the underworld, and may have added considerable strength to the intelligence unit in its war against crime.

Each intelligence officer should be keenly aware of these facts. *The creation of an image of omnipresence or all-knowing in the hoodlum mind has definite value in controlling organized crime.* In this area, rumor has a particular tactical application.

Among other things, the anatomy of a rumor includes such things as emotional appeal, logical appeal, a grain of truth, and a willing carrier. After the intelligence unit is fairly well established, a casual remark by one of its members made to some gangster can create all sorts of havoc for the hoodlums. Likewise, a brief story extolling unusual accomplishments of any particular member of the unit will also strengthen the entire unit. In this sense, the unit engages in a form of psychological warfare against criminals.

SCOPE OF INTELLIGENCE OPERATIONS

One of the most effective municipal police intelligence agencies in the United States reports that their scope of operations is as follows: (Their report has been purposely sanitized.)

The intelligence division is responsible for gathering information and investigation of all phases of organized crime. This includes individuals who, by their previous associations or suspected endeavors, constitute a potential hazard to society. In addition to the commonly classified vice activities, rackets, both in the field of labor and bunco, are found to be a lucrative endeavor in this group.

The primary purpose of this division is to gather information; it is not an enforcement unit. Very few arrests are made and, wherein possible, information is given to an enforcement unit of the department. That unit effects the arrest, conducts subsequent investigation and court proceedings. Officers of the intelligence division cooperate and are, at times, loaned to complete the investigation. Our objective is obtained when an activity is broken up and our effectiveness is considerably increased by the intelligence division officers not being identified with such operation. We work closely with other agencies, both local, state and federal, and are not confined to geographical boundaries in our investigations but try to consider the problem as it affects the welfare of the city.

Officers usually work in pairs and each team is assigned a vehicle equipped with triplex radio. Each team is assigned the responsibility of continual coverage on a group of known hoodlums. These officers are further responsible for maintaining the individual dossier file on each of the assigned characters. All officers are required to be on the alert for other individuals whose past histories indicate a lack of legitimate enterprise. Close scrutiny is maintained whenever possible on this type of person. The primary purpose of close surveillance is to prevent the individual from making hoodlum contacts and from making any illegitimate money while he is being obviously under observation. While this technique is expensive in manpower outlay, it is quite successful when used from time to time.

Since we are charged with the responsibility of obtaining information on organized crime, it is necessary that our officers be particularly adapted to obtaining and maintaining sources of information. However, we will not tolerate any fraternization with underworld characters and departmental regulations prohibit any officer from accepting for his personal use any gratuities or rewards. All such contributions must be turned over to the fire and police pension fund or general fund of the city.

Four sergeants devote full time to "background checking," i.e., credit reports, bank information, utilities and others, as we are constantly attempting to establish association between known characters or infiltration of known hoodlums into legitimate business. The division maintains a seven-man detail at the airport, covering twenty hours per day. These men are especially selected for ability to remember names and faces and are there to observe all incoming and outgoing hoodlums. A daily report of their observations is forwarded, through supervisors, to the files.

We maintain our own electronics crew to make dictating-machine installations as provided by state law and a considerable amount of information is obtained in this manner. We, likewise, maintain our own supply of tape recorders and necessary paraphernalia.

Personnel investigations, normally, are not handled by this division. Those instances wherein police personnel are suspected of being allied with hoodlums are taken up with the division of internal affairs and subsequent investigation may be handled by either or both divisions.

The intelligence division maintains its own filing system and all files therein are the property of the Chief of Police, not official police records, and are not subject to subpoena, as outlined in the Code of Civil Procedure. These files are not open to perusal by members of the department; however, officers are encouraged to consult this division whenever they are interested in an individual identified in our files. The files are cross-indexed with the general criminal files of the department and we are desirous of assisting anyone seeking information in an investigation. However, this is accomplished by the desk officer of the division ascertaining the type of information desired and making a file search and furnishing same. Perusal of a file is subject to the approval of the division commander and can be countermanded only by the Chief of Police. An alphabetical master card file is maintained on all persons who have been brought to our attention. For this file we use a 5 x 8 card which contains space for name, physical description, photograph, various police numbers, addresses, phones, description and license of car, location, friendly activities and association. The back of the card is used for posting of all reports wherein subject's name is mentioned. It might be well to point out that we require officers to make written reports on all information and observation. Likewise, a code is used to identify sources of information, which code is confidential between the reporting officer and the commander. We continually stress that information must be recorded so that officers ten years hence may have the benefit of past activities and operations of these individuals.

In addition to dossier files on the more prominent hoodlums, reports are filed by subject matter and a second copy filed chronologically. The following 3 x 5 size files are kept:

1. A building file, wherein credit reports have been obtained on businesses suspected of being connected in organized crime.
2. An address file gives the known addresses of all subjects.
3. A telephone number file of all individuals and businesses.
4. An automobile file containing license number and description of the cars operated by those persons of interest to this division.
5. An alphabetical file maintained on registered bookmakers.

One further operation is the subscription to and news clipping of some twenty-three metropolitan newspapers throughout the United States. We distribute news items to the specialized units such as robbery, burglary, narcotics, etc. These items on racketeers and prominent hoodlums are indexed and filed in this office.

Selection of Intelligence Objectives

Total capability of the intelligence unit and priority are the two principal considerations in the selection of intelligence objectives. The outcome of any intelligence endeavor is usually related to the number of personnel available and to their combined and separate abilities. All staff requests must take this into account.

Staff priority requests must be realistic with respect to the unit workload at any given time. What would be too great a burden at one moment may not be at another. This seems to be another reason why the intelligence unit must have staff representation at all times.

It logically arises, what is priority and what is not? Anything which could have a major detrimental effect on the community or the department is well within the meaning. The majority of staff requests will be more concerned with short term problems. The intelligence unit should not sacrifice their long-term projects in attempting to meet all of these demands.

CHAPTER SEVEN

INTERROGATION

What to look for in this chapter . . .

A review of basic interrogation;
The logical appeal in interrogation;
The emotional appeal in interrogation;
Some special techniques of interrogation;
Intelligence interrogation, formal vs. informal interrogation.

I F a person had to select several of the defining areas within law enforcement, there is little doubt that the ability to conduct a good interrogation would be one of the first considerations. Interrogation is an art, or perhaps even a science. It separates excellence from mediocrity among law enforcement personnel. Though our principal purpose in this chapter is to explore some of the aspects of interrogation as they apply to intelligence operations, necessity and importance indicate a review of basic interrogation is in order.

BASIC INTERROGATION

The principal variable factor in interrogation is the "subject," the person being interrogated. Subjects can be classified in many different ways, namely by motives, intelligence, personalities, emotions, and several other factors. The approach to any interrogation is not only governed by these factors, it is also influenced by the subject's relationship to the instant case, e.g., suspect, witness, victim, or informant.

The ability to conduct a good interrogation is closely akin to the degree of experience the interrogator possesses, however, not totally neglecting formal training and education. The personal and professional experiences, genetic endowment, and moral standards of the interrogator will also come into operation and influence during an interrogation.

Preparation prior to the actual interrogation is one aspect of basic interrogation that is too often neglected by police officers. All good preparation includes the learning of all background data regarding the subject, plus the complete details regarding the incident in question. Though many interrogations are "played by ear," good preparations should include a physical and mental plan or procedure.

Today the mental plan must, by edict of the Supreme Court in their ruling in *Miranda vs Arizona*, include a warning to any suspect regarding his rights. If this warning is made into a ritual, it can create impassible barriers. Proof of the warning is best accomplished by a signed statement.

Momentarily disregarding special techniques, basic interrogation has two fundamental approaches, the logical approach and the emotional approach. The first is an appeal for cooperation based upon sound reasoning; the latter is an appeal for cooperation directed toward the emotions of the subject. Regardless of the approach, both involve the proper application of legally and socially approved pressure.

Before a logical appeal may be made, the interrogator must state that the purpose of most interrogations is to arrive at the truth. Though some will disagree, every suspect will "talk" if approached properly. We must concede that on occasion the proper approach may be very complex. In some suspect interrogations, lies become almost as valuable as truth.

Logical Appeal

Before a logical appeal may be made, the interrogator must establish that the subject is capable of logical thinking or reasoning. As a general rule, the logical appeal is less likely to produce results than the emotional appeal. The logical appeal also usually requires a much more extensive base of tangible evidence.

In employing the logical appeal, the interrogator should exhibit self-assurance and personal poise. His demeanor should indicate that he has no doubt whatsoever as to the outcome of the interrogation and that his main purpose in talking to the subject is to offer assistance to one whom circumstances has placed in a difficult position. The subject may be shown the futility of his resistance since the interrogator's objective will be met and the time of all concerned will be saved.

Where there is little doubt of the subject's guilt, the psychological manifestation of his emotional turmoil may be pointed out to him as expressions of his guilt. The psychological manifestations may include such things as dry mouth, rapid heart beat (visible by pulsations in neck veins), excessive perspiration, frequent changes in position, picking the clothing or ear lobes or lips, and red flushed appearance.

Emotional Appeal

Although no fixed formula exists for determining which subjects are best approached through an emotional appeal, a key to the problem may be found by considering the "conscience" or the "attitude" of the subject. It should be always borne in mind, however, a subject who is without a conscience, or possesses a very inferior one, cannot be reached by an emotional appeal based upon a consideration of the feelings and rights of others. He simply does not understand this feeling. If the subject's attitude predicates an emotional basis, a well-laid emotional appeal might be effective.

Some of the most common implements of the emotional appeal are related to love, hate, fear, and various combinations of the aforementioned. The adroit interrogator can effectively use one or all of these in an interrogation.

Where the emotion of love is involved, the interrogator may cause an unwilling subject to change his attitude by appealing to his love of wife, children, parents or others. To achieve results the subject should be shown that truth and cooperation are the only solutions to his predicament, if he is sincerely interested in the welfare of his loved ones. The degree of cooperation can be correlated to the degree and extent of his love.

When the preliminary phase of interrogation reveals a strong feeling of antagonism toward another individual, this can be often used to an advantage. Hate is usually often accompanied by a desire for vengence. It may be possible for the interrogator to indicate a manner in which this vengence can be satisfied. When hate is absent, it can be many times planted in the mind of a naive subject by implication, insinuation and innuendo.

There are many ways in which the emotion of fear may be utilized by the interrogator. Experience has shown that this is the emotion most readily induced where it does not already exist. As a general statement, when fear is present, some magnification is necessary, however, the interrogator should estimate the extent to which it should be magnified without rendering the subject incapable of confession.

The emotional appeal substantially involves a search by the interrogator for the necessary emotional stimulus which will evince the truth. This can be usually accomplished by forcing the subject into mental situations by questions or comments, the answers to which require reflection on an emotional area.

Whether the appeal is logical or emotional, the preliminary phase of either should include an irrelevant question period so that the interrogator will have a better opportunity to observe the truth telling style of the subject. Occasionally both logic and emotion will fail completely. When this happens, success can be achieved only through the use of special techniques. As a general rule, special techniques are employed only when other methods have failed. A wise interrogator must be constantly alert for situations wherein a special technique may be employed.

Above all, the interrogator should know exactly what he is going to do before undertaking the use of a special technique. He must consider the possible effect on the interrogation, himself, and the entire department, if the special technique fails.

Special Techniques

Special techniques can range from the typical to the complex. The complex may include such things as hypnosis, truth drugs, or even polygraph. The less dramatic techniques are usually used more often.

The "false incident" technique can have many modifications, however, it substantially involves the introduction of a false incident which requires the subject to affirm or deny its existence. It can be used to break an alibi or to force the subject into a false alibi.

The "honey-vinegar" technique, which is sometimes referred to as "sweet and sour," or "good-guy bad-guy," involves the application of a team of interrogators working together in a prearranged role. The procedure is based simply on the attitudes of the two interrogators. One assumes the pleasing, comforting role and the other is harsh, lacking in understanding, and quite critical. At the right time he usually becomes obnoxious and declares the guilt of the suspect. After becoming as obnoxious as permissible, he usually departs from the interrogation room and the other interrogator applies the "honey," the "honey" being consideration, understanding, sympathy and emphathy. To be successful in this technique, it is usually best applied at the average to below average intelligence level. For symbolic representation see Figure 7.1.

FIGURE 7.1.

"The split pair" technique is usually used when there are two or more suspects involved in a particular incident. It is simply divide and conquer, or pit one against the other, e.g., "He already told us all about it."

Again this is usually limited to first offenders and then only to subjects of lower mentality.

The "two by two" technique usually involves the questioning of a single subject by two teams of interrogators at separate intervals regarding two entirely different incidents. On occasion the subject will be unable to recall the details provided to each separate team, resulting from the different verbal stimulus.

The "false line-up" technique involves the placing of the suspect in a line-up where he can overhear preplanned tentative identification made by prop victims or witnesses. This technique can be effectively employed where there is high degree of certainty that the suspect is the person who committed the act in question.

There are probably as many special techniques as there are exceptionally skilled interrogators. Each interrogator will develop methods that are compatible with his personality. The one quality that all interrogators must possess is articulation, the ability to communicate. The majority of all interrogations that are successful usually develop a flow pattern that is smooth, unbroken and uninterrupted.

Interrogation requires that control be maintained at all times. The interrogator must be able to play many roles. The tools available to him are his words, his method of expression, and actions.

INTELLIGENCE INTERROGATIONS

One of the major problems in intelligence interrogations is the fact that on many occasions the interrogator must skillfully or adroitly conceal the true object of his probing or questions. To ask questions and yet conceal what you are seeking requires considerable experience, for almost every critical question conveys a hint as to what is being sought.

Oftentimes the intelligence officer must avoid such things as contrast and contiguity. If a series of questions are asked, flagrant contrasting questions must be avoided where protection of the topic of inquiry is essential. Questions out of context will be remembered by the subject. The same is true of questions that break contiguity.

Many times the intelligence officer will have to blanket the area of his probing with several related topics of a similar nature. By example, if we were seeking information regarding a man's brother, we could ask about father, mother, sisters, brothers and other kinfolk. This would not be totally effective in all cases, however, on most routine inquiries it will suffice.

Pretense Interrogations

Only the most skilled interrogators can master pretense interrogation or interviewing. In this type of interrogation, the subject is purposely led to believe, through a pretense, that the interrogator is seeking information of a particular nature when in fact it is something else. On occasion pretense interrogation will have as its sole purpose the generation of a false incident or rumor through the "grapevine." This can have sound tactical application in crime prevention.

Formal versus Informal Interrogation

In formal interrogation the subject is aware of the fact that he is being interrogated or interviewed. The opposite is true in informal interrogation; the subject is being interrogated without being aware of the fact.

Informal interrogation involves considerable planning, props, and an abundance of trained personnel. A typical example might be a party with the majority of those in attendance aimed at a specific single subject with each having a specific subtle conversational area to cover.

Planning this type of activity is critical. With security being the major consideration, each officer's area of probing must be carefully screened in advance. If officers cannot be used, operational informants can be effectively assigned to handle this activity.

A second application of informal interrogation seems worthy of mention. District or regional meetings of vice or narcotic law enforcement officers usually occur quarterly or at least semi-annually. Three or four intelligence teams in attendance, with specific assignments, can gather a considerable amount of data concerning conditions in surrounding communities that may eventually effect their own city.

CHAPTER EIGHT

INTELLIGENCE REPORTING AND RECORDS

What to look for in this chapter . . .

The basic considerations in police report writing;
Intelligence report writing;
Intelligence record cards and what they contain;
Intelligence records and indexing.

BASIC CONSIDERATIONS IN REPORT WRITING

O<small>NE</small> of the most important basic considerations of report writing is, of course, the language used. A simple word which is easily understood is by far the best. Police officers too often forget the meaning of the words of the author Ben Johnson who stated, "Language most shows a man, speak that I may see thee."

If something can be stated properly with less words, it should be done so. Brevity is an essential quality of a good report. Superfluous verbage contributes little to a factual police report.

Brevity does not alleviate the necessity for proper punctuation and accurate spelling. A person can be an outstanding investigator, however, if his spelling and punctuation indicates that of a fourth grade level, his ability and proficiency will also receive the same evaluation.

One of the most elementary rules of English construction is violated continually by many police officers. Every complete sentence must have at least one subject and one predicate. The best form of writing should normally include just a simple subject and a simple predicate. Although, there are occasions where it is necessary to create compound or complex constructions.

It is almost always necessary to paragraph any narrative report. A paragraph is simply a warning to the reader that a change in thought is about to occur, or that a new subject is about to be explored. Most paragraphs contain between fifty and one-hundred

141

words, although there are occasions where these may be shorter or longer. Failure to paragraph properly causes a tremendous waste of time, or in other terms, manpower.

Simply stated, the officer should write his report for the reader's benefit. The report should be complete, easily understandable, brief, and accurate. The police officer must write to inform, not to impress.

Preparations for Report Writing

To write a concise and complete report on the first attempt, many officers will be required to first review and organize their notes. An outline can be drawn quickly from the known facts of any case, particularly, if it follows a chronological sequence. After the outline is identified, the officer should inspect it for completeness prior to engaging the actual writing of the report. The outline should answer the questions when and where, who did what, how and why.

There are basically two types of police reports, the narrative and the modus operandi. For narrative report writing there are several basic components which are as follows:

1. Title or subject of the incident.
2. Date and time of occurrence.
3. Predication (authority and cause of the report)
4. File number
5. Synopsis (for long report only)
6. Body of report (the answers to when and where, who did what, how and why).
7. Disposition of the case.
8. Opinions of the author when relevant.
9. Author's name.

The modus operandi report is usually dependent upon an existing form within the particular agency. Modus operandi reports have a number of uses, however, one of the principle uses is to identify the criminal by his way of working or method of operation. Modus operandi reports may be very extensive, however, they must essentially include the following: apparent motive, trademark, object of attack, method, type of victim, type of area, vehicles, weapons, instruments of attack and conversation used.

Modus operandi reports are based on the theory that a criminal will repeat those habits or methods which have given him success in the past. Some criminals constantly change their pattern, this in itself is a modus operandi.

Purpose of Reports

One major reason for reports is that a factual description of a crime, a complaint, or strategic information is permanently recorded for future use. Reports written when facts are fresh in the minds of witnesses and the reporting officers are more reliable. Man's memory tends to fade with time and intervening life experiences.

Reports are of important aid in the administration of justice. Police reports provide the necessary information for the prosecutor, the judge and the probation and parole agencies. Final adjudication is many times dependent on the police officer's original report.

The officers' reports also provide a basis for future statistical data required by management. The information may be of traffic classification that may be needed to reduce traffic accidents. It may contain facts concerning needed traffic control devices or data essential to selective enforcement. It may provide the necessary information needed for field deployment of policemen to prevent various crimes. Collectively, they may also reveal weaknesses in present police field tactics.

INTELLIGENCE REPORT WRITING

The same basic considerations that apply to narrative reports also apply to intelligence reports. There is, however, divergence from agency to agency with respect to form. For example, some agencies require all paragraphs to be numbered consecutively within each dossier, others do not. Some agencies permit only one lead to be listed in one paragraph, others have no provisions for this. Several agencies require five or six spaces be left blank between paragraphs for ease in duplication, lead inventory, and control.

Some agencies which maintain intelligence dossiers on major hoodlums do so in accordance with a specific format. These formats will vary in form, however, they usually include substantially the same categories, e.g. complete description, addresses, telephones, vehicles, criminal history, associates, places frequented, past activities, current enterprises, etc. The majority of this information is recorded on specific forms rather than in narrative reports.

Most intelligence reports containing information received from informants and liaison sources are completed in narrative form. An example of the body of a report giving information received from an informant reads as follows:

> On 30 June 1967, T-14, who has provided reliable information in the past, stated substantially the following concerning the bombing of Sam's Florist Shop, 921 W. 14th Street, this city, on 29 June 1967.

001 At approximately 2215 hours, 29 June 1967, an unknown white male entered the Florist Shop, carrying a small brown suitcase.

002 At approximately 2218 hours the same man exited the shop, without the suitcase; got into a car parked at the curb and drove west on 14th Street.

003 At approximately 2222 hours an explosion "virtually leveled the florist shop." No one else had entered or exited the shop in the past 10 minutes.

004 Descriptions:

> *SUSPECT:* White male, 30 to 35 years, 5'8" to 5'10", 160 to 170 lbs, black wavy hair, medium build, olive complexion, appeared to be of Italian descent. Wearing a black turtle neck sweater and black trousers.
>
> *VEHICLE:* Buick, 1967, 4 door Sedan, light blue, California license # AZY131. Left tail light not working.
>
> *SUITCASE:* Medium brown, approx 26 inches by 14 inches by 8 inches. Appeared to be new.

005 At approximately 1300 hours 21 June 1967 (seven days prior) the above described SUSPECT was observed having lunch with Rito Venouese (See file O/C 003) at John's Cafe, 114 E. Main Street, this city. This fact and SUSPECT'S actions of looking back over his shoulder when leaving the florist shop called specific attention to HIM.

006 . . . .

In the above narrative report the reader's attention is directed to the following features:

1. The report contains a preamble describing when the information was received; the source is identified by code for security and a general comment is made regarding the source's reliability.
2. Excluding the preamble, each paragraph is numbered and each contains one investigative lead. Numbering paragraphs permits rapid reference to particular items in lengthy reports. It also permits easy construction of a lead inventory to guide supervision.
3. The report is simply a chronological sequence of what the source observed. It usually begins with the answer to the questions, when, where, and who.
4. The bombing would receive a specific index classification by subject matter, depending upon the decimal system used by the particular agency.
5. The report may contain the true name of the author or it may contain a coded symbol or number assigned to the officer.
6. All subsequent inquiries regarding the incident would have the paragraphs numbered beginning where the numbers ended in this report.

INTELLIGENCE RECORDS

The extent and diversity of intelligence records will vary from agency to agency depending on staff needs and manpower allotments. Typical records usually include a master or alpha reference file, a telephone number file, a vehicle file, and a building and/or address file.

Master Reference File

Normally all personalities and organizations are entered separately on 5" x 8" cards and filed alphabetically. The content and arrangement of the material on each card is optional; however, most agencies include such items as, a current photograph of the subject, the complete name and descriptive data, all police identification numbers in addition to other identification numbers such as social security and driver's license, addresses (past and present), telephone numbers (home and business), known associates, criminal history, behavior characteristics, and the vehicles which the subject may own or have immediate access to.

The reverse side of the master card usually contains one-line summaries regarding each individual intelligence report that contains any reference to the subject. This permits a rapid search in summary form regarding any particular person or organization.

The master card lends itself to machine processing. The coding of the various items will permit rapid sorting and selection. At present, most agencies use a manual search system for the master file as well as all the entries on each card. The near future may bring machine processing of the various items contained in the master cards, including the summaries on the reverse side.

The master reference card is the heart or core of the intelligence records system. As a result of this fact, access to this file must be limited. A misfiled card for all practical purposes is lost forever.

Decimal System

Intelligence reports, as previously mentioned, are categorized according to subject matter e.g., bookmaking, extortion, narcotics, prostitution, mafia, etc. Any numbering system may be used. The common system is a simple decimal arrangement involving the use of two or three decimals. By example 1.3.67 could be used to designate bookmaking in a particular city in the year 1967. The methods used by different cities vary greatly, however, it is mainly a different arrangement of generally the same subject matter. Major categories with some of the subcategories may be arranged as follows:

1. Bookmaking
   1.1 Current information on subject.
   1.2 Individual rundowns.
   1.3 Information other cities.
   1.4 Information other states.
   1.5 etc.
   1.6 etc.
2. Bribery
   2.1 Current information on subject.
   2.2 Individual rundown.
   2.3 Information other cities.
   2.4 Information other states.
   2.5 etc.
   2.6 etc.

3. Extortion
   3.1 Current information of subject.
   3.2 Individual rundowns.
   3.3 Information other cities.
   3.4 Information other states.
   3.5   etc.
   3.6   etc.
4. Gambling
   4.1 Current information on subject.
   4.2 Individual rundowns.
   4.3 Information other cities.
   4.4 Information other states.
   4.5 Lotteries
      4.51 Chinese lotteries
      4.52 Italian lotteries
      4.53 Irish lotteries

Other major categories may include such things as Narcotics, Labor Racketeering, Mafia, Nomadic Hoodlums, Subversives, etc. The important thing to remember is that when the file is first established that it is made sufficiently broad enough to cover the potential major areas of activities.

Telephone Number File

A telephone number file provides rapid access to telephone numbers of personalities and organizations that may be of intelligence interest. It also saves duplication once the registered owner of an unlisted number is obtained. Telephone numbers can be conveniently indexed by using the last three or four digits and filing these numerically. Almost every person possesses a list of telephone numbers that he is more likely to use. Acquisition of this data, coupled with a telephone number file, can lead to significant intelligence information.

Vehicle File

In today's highly mobile society, the commission of almost every crime involves the use of a vehicle. With this premise in mind it becomes apparent that intelligence units must develop methods to identify people through vehicles. A typical vehicle file can be established by using the letters or numerals or both. One such method commonly utilizes the last three digits of the license number. Some also include the color and make of the vehicle.

Structure and/or Address File

Certain locations of businesses and residence have greater intelligence value than others. As a result, some agencies establish a cross-reference file on all addresses that come to their attention in intelligence matters of high priority. Thus when certain personalities elude surveillance, or when intelligence personnel are seeking the location of a particular subject, lead data is readily available.

CHAPTER NINE

CRIME PREVENTION

What to look for in this chapter . . .

Who has the responsibility for crime prevention?
How is crime prevented?
What is the intelligence contribution?

Crime Prevention Defined

In its broadest application it seems permissible to claim that crime prevention includes the elimination of the desire and opportunity to commit a crime. The various reasons that individuals may have for committing crimes are probably as numerous as the opportunities they observe.

In a strict sense, crime prevention has little relation to intelligence activity other than being a by-product. There are, however, some instances which intelligence actions may be exclusively crime prevention. Timely collection of certain data can prevent the maturation of criminal schemes or plans, thus saving citizens from major financial and physical injuries.

Why some people commit crime is anybody's guess. In other cases, it seems easy to understand. Sociologists and psychologists offer many different theories; many have little validity, others may have a thread of importance. Too often these theories originate from observations made in the laboratory rather than in the concrete and steel jungle where man can be at his worst.

The answer to why a person commits a crime may contain part of the answer to crime prevention; however, the authors are more concerned with the responsibilties rather than some of the subtle causes. From the standpoint of personal observations only, the most consistent common denominator for all criminals is truancy from school during the puberal years. We realize that it logically arises, why were these people truants? No doubt the answers would fill volumes.

RESPONSIBILITIES FOR CRIME PREVENTION

The final success or failure for crime prevention is a question of responsibility. To achieve any degree of accomplishment, total society must be keyed to the problem. Stress must be placed on individual, business, police, and community responsibilities.

Individual Responsibility

When the deviants and deviates among us continue multiplying in number, forming unions, and holding regular meetings, our way of life is in jeopardy. Many of our youth tend to live as if adolescence was a last fling at life, rather than a preparation for it. The fifteen and sixteen year old group commits more serious crimes than any other group.

Each mature individual must accept his responsibility to en-encourage wayward youth to change loyalties from one that encompasses filth and immorality to one of dignity and consideration of others. But, this is where the problem is; too many are too busy, frightened, or indifferent; too many are not convinced themselves.

Many individuals forget that silence in the knowledge of public wrongdoing makes the indifferent observer as morally responsible as the wrongdoer. Yet, no one wants to get involved.

Many people wonder, just what is a responsible individual. We say that he may be the man who runs toward a car accident to render aid and testify in court. He may be the doctor or nurse who stops at the scene to assist, knowing that they may be sued later by the victim or relatives of the victim. He may be the individual who stopped to pick up the discarded candy wrapper to throw it in the trash can. Or, it may be the man who runs into the dark alley to assist a screaming woman. He may be the truck driver at the roadside stand who warns three beer-happy teenagers to stop swearing or that he will personally throw them out of the cafe.

Business Responsibility

The business owner is usually a taxpayer of some import. As such, he certainly has the right to question whether the police department is effectively and efficiently carrying out its responsibilities to him and the community. Yet, in his position as a major taxpayer he sometimes forgets his responsibility. Has he provided reasonable security and protection for his own property? Has he been fair with his fellow taxpayers, or has he by his negligence, omissions, or apathy required a disproportionate share of the police services available and paid for, not just by him, but by all of the taxpayers.

The business owner has the responsibility for providing good physical security of his premises. He must increase the time needed to gain illegal entry. Proper locking devices, in conjunction with adequate internal and external lighting, are essential in the execution of this responsibility.

Police Responsibilities

Proceeding on the assumption that we will never reach the position that we can say that we have all of the policemen we need, it becomes absolutely essential that police enlist, as an active participating ally, the generally apathetic but law-abiding majority of the community.

Frequent inspection of the business premises and preventive patrol are the traditional methods of police crime prevention. Present rising crime trends indicate that something more than traditional methods may be needed. Crime rate is outgrowing population increases at a ratio of at least four to one.

In some cities the application of modern technology is becoming apparent; yet, for the most part, law enforcement is not utilizing techniques and methods available to combat the rising crime in our streets. By example, the fundamentals of intelligence data processing and use are still a number of years in the future for most cities.

When we can predict when and where crimes will occur and probably who will commit them, then police will be in a position to more efficiently carry out their role in crime prevention. Without the application of intelligence concepts and practices, this will never be accomplished.

Community Responsibilities

Every community must insist that the police, city government, and other organizations each assume their responsibilities for crime prevention. Only when people, other than the victims of crimes, raise their voices in indignation will we ever be successful. Each community group should contribute to the proper attitude necessary for effective crime prevention.

SCHOOLS: What we teach in our schools is quite important; however, what we fail to teach may be just as important. If we fail for just one generation to teach our children respect for law and order, our system may vanish forever.

When our educators permit unbecoming conduct and attitudes to flourish in the schools, our crime prevention attempts are slated for less than mediocrity. Inconsistent and passive discipline breeds an attitude in youth that lends itself to a lack of respect for the rights and property of others. Unnecessary absenteeism and truancy are usually always present in any typical criminal behavior pattern. Schools can and must play a significant role in crime prevention.

CITY GOVERNMENT: Though there are many things that city government can to do in the field of crime prevention, several seem more important than the rest. Among these, anti-crime legislation, sufficient police manpower, and active programs which generate support for law enforcement are predominant.

Anti-burglary legislation, which has as its central theme, locking and lighting requirements for business establishments, is one example of anti-crime legislation. Cities such as Detroit, Chicago, Kansas City, Houston, and Gary, Indiana, indicate that street lighting is an important crime prevention tool. Oakland, California, coupled business security in the form of particular locking requirements, coupled with lighting, and found the crime prevention value very gratifying.

Chattanooga, Tennessee, had a twelve block area with a fantastic homicide rate. The city flooded the area with light, the crimes of violence were cut 70 to 90 per cent. In Austin, Texas, new lighting cut some categories of crime 90 per cent.

A street lighting program in Flint, Michigan, cut felonies 60 per cent in the downtown area. "The new street lighting helped decrease crime beyond our expectations," says Police Chief George Paul.

McPherson, Kansas, has installed one of the most extensive street lighting programs in the United States. Brightness was increased six times and enough street lights added so that there is now one for every two and one-half homes. There have been no burglaries since then. Chief Paul Smith states "Our lights have just about illuminated residential crime out of existence."

Traffic accidents can be equated to crime. As traffic accidents in most cities begin to rise, patrol time decreases; as patrol time decreases, opportunity for the potential criminal increases. Therefore, it appears that traffic enforcement, education, and engineering are related to crime prevention. When police management is denied an adequate safe margin in manpower allocations they enter into a cycle that excludes sufficient time for crime prevention programs. Perhaps erroneously, most police agencies favor putting more patrolmen on the street to handle demands from the public, rather than establishing crime prevention bureaus within their respective departments.

In terms of awakening a true sense of citizen responsibility for crime prevention, city government can embark upon programs which generate support for law enforcement. A climate of respect for law and order complements the programs aimed specifically to prevent criminal acts.

Almost any program, which has as its goal the prevention of crime, will be heralded by police as a worthy effort. Any crime prevention program naturally connotes a support for law enforcement. Some programs can be designed exclusively for supporting police and judicial activities. The salient features of this type of program might include the following:

1. Never forget policemen are the sons of good citizens like yourself. They are human beings. Be as quick to compliment as you are to criticize; however, do not be afraid to report dishonest acts by police officers to police management.
2. Do not criticize all police for the poor judgment of one officer. He, like yourself, can make mistakes.
3. Encourage good pay for police officers. This permits police administrators to compete in the labor market. Remember you usually get just what you pay for.
4. Talk with policemen. Learn their problems and needs. Encourage them to join and speak to your civic organizations. You will be surprised what you can learn about your community.

5. Oppose police review boards; they are part of a design to cripple effective law enforcement. Besides, police are constantly reviewed by the news media, Federal Bureau of Investigation, Attorney General, Grand Jury, District Attorney, City Attorney, City Council, the Courts, and by their own police Internal Affairs Divisions.

6. At the voting polls, protect the merit system. Do not permit Civil Service Personnel Boards to be replaced by politically appointed referees. Labor to keep politics out of the police department.

7. Beware of false claims of police brutality and false claims of civil rights violations. Do not equate legal and necessary force with brutality. Inquire by asking police management. It is your right and duty.

8. Let the judges you elect know they have your support in the administration of criminal justice. Assist the prosecutor if called upon.

9. Report and bear witness against all criminals. Also, never forget the two dollar bet supports organized crime. Help eliminate it by non-participation and prompt reporting.

10. Teach your children respect for policemen by your own example. Insist that your schools actively reinforce this teaching. When a young policeman violates his oath, maybe his parents contributed by their failure to properly instill the same principles as you are now doing.

When city government pursues an active program designed to prevent crime, they should also consider the business licensing aspects. Most cities require all businesses to obtain a city business license. An alert informed licensing staff can have a very pronounced influence on the prevention of organized crime entering into any city.

Insurance Companies

Insurance companies are in a rather unique position, particularly those companies that insure businesses, homes, and automobiles. Their position is unique in that they can have a subtle influence on attitudes essential in crime prevention, not to mention their legislative lobbying power.

Just suppose what the effect on commercial burglary would be if insurance companies insisted that external rear lighting was a mandatory requirement prior to issuing a protective policy to a business owner. Or, further suppose what the result would be if there was an enforced law which required vehicles parked on public streets to be locked during certain hours of darkness. Or, what would happen to criminal offenders if the insurance companies, through the courts, insisted on restitution.

HOW POLICE CAN PREVENT CRIME

It all depends upon what type of crime we are talking about. Crimes may range from petty theft to large swindles, from bunco and bribery to the large cartels of organized crime. Traditional police methods will effectively counter some of them while failing in the others. Police are presently not structured or organized to combat those crimes other than the typical individually offensive acts usually committed by one or several criminals. And as indicting as it sounds, nationally, the police only clear 25 to 30 per cent of these crimes, on the average.

Seeking Assistance

One major reason why the police fail to prevent crime is that they do not actively seek the assistance of the community organizations and individuals available. The responsibility for seeking this assistance is left undone or permitted to slide without accountability in most police agencies. A crime prevention coordinator or staff officer who actively seeks the assistance of community forces is, without further discussion, critical to effective police operations.

With adequate manpower and reasonable Supreme Court decisions, applying traditional patrol and inspection methods, police can cope with the typical community crime problems. However, most agencies today do not have adequate manpower; the Supreme Court has lost its sense of purpose; and the community crime problems are not typical, particularly the ratio of crimes committed to the number of policemen available to solve them, or prevent them.

Part of the solution is quite obvious. We must have more policemen, or relief legislation to overcome the Supreme Court's recent decisions, or more community participation in crime prevention. Perhaps all three are the answer.

Seeking assistance must be a continuing effort well planned and directed. Many things can be done by the police. Soliciting drug stores to report the purchases of #5 gelatin capsules by nonprofessional people, is one such effort. These capsules are commonly used in the narcotic traffic; reporting their purchases to the police will have little or no effect on the narcotic traffic.

However, it will identify and focus police enforcement attention on those currently active. The druggist need only obtain a license number after the purchase of the capsules and after the subject has departed from the store. The premise is sound; every addict has a "hustle" or scheme to obtain money to buy dope; this scheme is usually a criminal act such as theft or burglary. Early identification and apprehension prevents crime.

Cooperation from service station owners should be sought. Inexpensive vibrating tools can be issued to mark hubcaps and other auto accessories, at no cost to the customer, with the customer's license number. This, coupled with a favorable press relations program, can have a pronounced affect on the theft of auto parts accessories.

Local radio and television stations will assist in broadcasting crime prevention warnings, if solicited. These broadcasts can be aimed at changing troublesome problems. These broadcasting stations will assist, but only if the police go to them.

Recognition of Some Methods of Entry

In addition to seeking assistance from various people, police must actively develop a security consciousness among merchants. While stressing internal and external lighting conditions, locking deficiencies must also be called to the attention of the proprietor. Many business owners believe that their locking systems are effective when in fact they are little or nothing in the way of security. It is the purpose of the following illustrations to point out how relatively simple it is for the experienced criminal to open typical locking mechanisms. The rookie policeman must also be aware of this.

When future discovery of the entry is of no consequence, a burglar will usually pry the door (as illustrated in Fig. 9.1) or break the bolt seat with brute force. On nonmetal door frames the only effective delay is two different locking points on the same door. This will not prevent entry, but it will discourage many because of the time delay factor and inconvenience.

Any locking bolt that can be opened with a shove knife, hook knife, or piece of plastic, should be avoided. Any amateur with little or no practice can open this locking device (see Figs. 9.2,

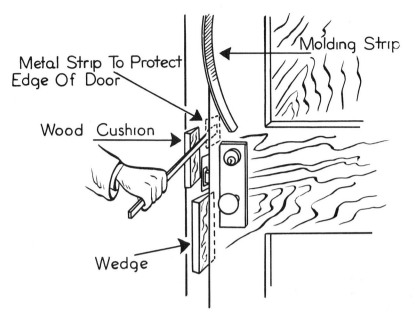

Molding Strip

Metal Strip To Protect
Edge Of Door

Wood Cushion

Wedge

FIGURE 9.1.

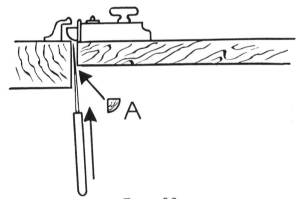

A

FIGURE 9.2.

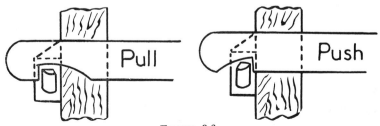

Pull

Push

FIGURE 9.3.

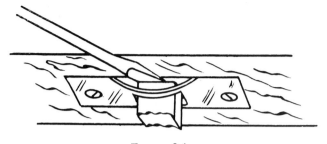

FIGURE 9.4.

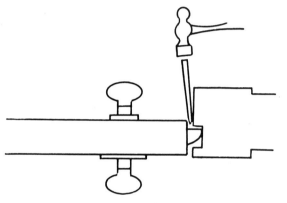

FIGURE 9.5.

9.3, and 9.10). When a burglar cannot slide the locking bolt he may cut it with a hammer and chisel as indicated in Figure 9.5.

It is only a minor effort to wrap a piece of friction tape around the retaining ring on many locks and then uscrew the ring with a small pipe wrench. After removing the ring, the entire lock can be simply slipped out of its recess. The index finger can reach the bolt and slide it to the rear, thus opening the door (see Figs. 9.6 and 9.7).

Many locking devices for windows have a rotating wing nut. These are usually opened by the use of a "slip knife" or piano wire and hand drill in combination. Figures 9.8 and 9.9 illustrate the more common application of these impliments.

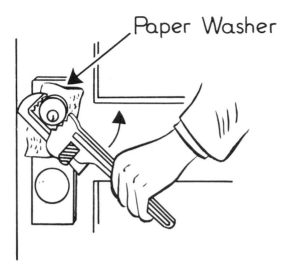

FIGURE 9.6.

FIGURE 9.7.

Figure 9.11 portrays the use of "hacksaw scissors" to turn a sliding bolt used on most rear doors of businesses in the smaller communities. The scissors, made from a hacksaw blade, will grasp the steel bolt and turn it or move it in any desired direction.

There are many methods available to open doors and windows regardless of the lock used. The rule that develops is easily stated, "the better the locking system, the longer it will take for the person to gain illegal access." There is no known locking device that can prevent a burglar from gaining entry into a business; however, the better the locking system, the longer it will take for entry. This delay increases the opportunity for apprehension.

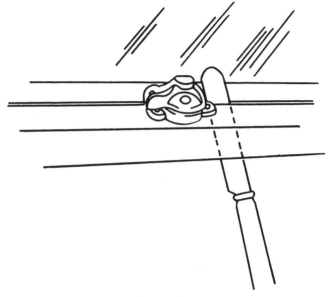

FIGURE 9.8.

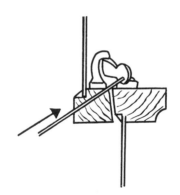

FIGURE 9.9.

Police Reserve Organizations for Crime Prevention

In seeking active assistance from different segments of the community, one method of integrating business and professional people into an effective crime prevention program, is through the police reserve organization. The potential in this area is almost

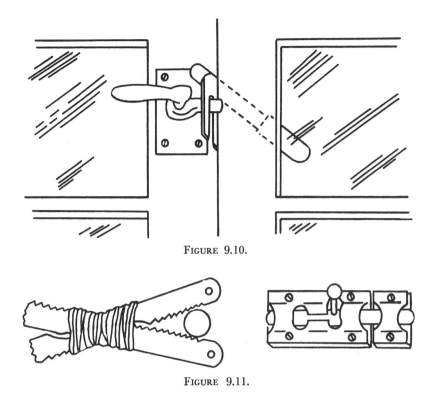

FIGURE 9.10.

FIGURE 9.11.

untapped in many communities. What can be better for crime prevention than to integrate and train business owners in how to better protect their own establishments. The degree of training and formality can vary according to community needs and staff desires.

A police reserve corps comprised of various industrial specialists can provide technical assistance at little or no expense to municipal police. Part of these specialists could include members of the press and public relations firms. Their knowledge in mass communication will prove very valuable in gaining public support for crime prevention programs.

THE INTELLIGENCE CONTRIBUTION

Focusing enforcement activities upon organized crime and subversives is one of the more obvious crime prevention aspects of intelligence. Breaking up plans and schemes of the hoodlum hierarchy is certainly prevention and protection of the lives and property of the citizenry.

Gathering information which provides the necessary leads for enforcement units is preventive in that the activities of the criminals would continue without the data being provided. The constant belief that technical surveillance is being employed, plus the obvious presence of overt surveillance, definitely restricts and prevents criminal actions.

With the proper image created, the mere fact that the intelligence unit is in existence, has a crime prevention quality. Hoodlums develop an aversion to cities that have active intelligence units, and rightly so. They never really know when they will become the target of law enforcement's penetrating eye.

As opposed to defense, intelligence is an offensive operation. Early discovery is one of the prime goals. Consequently, the active search for data relating to crime helps to spread a veil of imminent discovery over the heads of certain criminals, thus many times discouraging maturation of criminal schemes.

CHAPTER TEN

ADMINISTRATION OF THE INTELLIGENCE UNIT

What to look for in this chapter ...

How large should the intelligence unit be?
Who should serve and how are they selected?
How should the unit be organized?
Who should the Unit Commander report to?
Is supervision of intelligence personnel different?
Budget preparation;
The security aspects of intelligence operations;
Training intelligence personnel.

SIZE OF THE AGENCY VS. SIZE OF THE UNIT

Being an infant branch of the police service, not many comments can be found on just how large or small an intelligence unit should be. There is considerable debate on just how large the entire police department should or should not be. *Municipal Police Administration,* published by the International Association of City Managers, reflects that most police agencies of cities with populations of over twenty-five thousand, vary in size from .5 to 3.0 policemen per one thousand people. Some authorities give thought to the fact that intelligence units may have one per cent of the total personnel within this heirarchy.

Some important considerations in establishing the size of the intelligence unit include, overall size of the agency, metropolitan aspects, and the estimated infiltration of organized crime and other related aspects. Unfortunately, this latter category is difficult to evaluate without the unit being in existence. After the intelligence unit is formalized, organized crime comes under greater scrutiny; an expansion of coverage is not necessarily a demonstration of Parkinson's Law in action.

Pfiffner and Sherwood in their text, *Administrative Organization*, summarize Parkinson's Law as being substantially, "That the number of workers increases irrespective of the work to be done, that superiors create subordinate positions to enhance their own status, and that people in an expanding organization create unneeded tasks for each other." Initially, an intelligence unit may be created with only one or two or more personnel assigned. With the discovery of organized crime infiltration into local government and business, the unit may have to be increased greatly. An overly defensive attitude or fear of Parkinson's implied warning is not many times warranted.

In agencies that have a complement of several thousand policemen, the recommended one percent assignment of personnel to the intelligence unit can be effectively debated. The number must be consistent with the need of the staff to be properly informed in matters of major consequence. In most cases today, police administrators are required to make decisions with many important factors veiled in obscurity. If more personnel are needed to lift this veil, why not assign them? A correct decision with less personnel available to execute it, is far better than an incorrect decision with an abundance of personnel available.

PERSONNEL SELECTION

Selection of the intelligence division commander by the chief of police is probably one of the most important tasks to be performed. Coupled with other attributes, loyalty is paramount, however, loyalty should never be confused with blind obedience. The two are grossly different.

Though the chief will never find one with all the traits he is seeking, prime consideration should be given to that staff member who is not a "yes" man. He must be a person who consistently acts to provide truth, unshadowed, and in its simplest form regardless of personalities involved.

We could discuss traits of men for several volumes. Such things as honesty, integrity, interest, intelligence, academic respectability, poise, articulation, tact, and others are important. Yet, they are important for all policemen. What traits do we seek that are particularly important for intelligence personnel? How do we measure these traits? The typical tools are available and usually include comparative line performance, seniority, examinations, and trial on the job.

Though service in the intelligence unit should be a career assignment, no test or series of tests can measure fitness for any position to the same degree as actual trial on the job. Therefore, temporary assignments to this unit, for a reasonable testing period, appear to have considerable merit. Once a man has demonstrated the desirable performance and traits, it should be made a permanent assignment so long as good production and personal conduct are maintained.

Once the chief has appointed the intelligence commander, he should at the same time give the commander wide latitude in selecting the personnel for this unit. Again, loyalty to the chief and to the agency plays a major role, perhaps only surpassed by personal and professional integrity.

One method of trait identification to be used in the selection of intelligence personnel can be expressed as the four "I's," *interest* in this type of work, *ingenuity, integrity,* and a high degree of *intelligence* and the capacity for recall. A man who has little interest in this type of work, one who cannot rapidly improvise or adapt to a rapidly changing situation, and one whose price of betrayal may be purchasable is a threat to the entire intelligence family. But how do you measure these items?

A pre-assignment investigation of personnel, conducted by the staff or supervisors within the intelligence unit, is definitely an insurance policy that few can afford not to have. This could appropriately be classified as a counterintelligence activity. The intelligence commander cannot afford to have average policemen with average shortcomings. The candidate cannot be indiscreetly verbose, be dangerously in debt, or engage in adultery. Only the best may serve. Each must be a potential intelligence division commander.

The selection of personnel for service within the intelligence unit must also include an assessment of police maturity. Normally, it is desirable to select men who have had prior experience in vice or homicide investigations. The former are well acquainted with the use of undercover agents and informants; the latter are routinely accustomed to considerably detailed inquiries. This does not imply the exclusion of others.

In those agencies where a pre-employment background investigation is not conducted, a different problem is present. A background investigation is mandatory for all personnel assigned to intelligence activities due to the sensitive nature of the task. This background inquiry should include an exploration of the following:

> **Birth**—when, where, parents, family histories
> **Employment**—all places of employment and former supervisors and work histories
> **Military service**—branch, type of discharge, history of service
> **Organizations**—memberships, sponsors of introduction
> **References**—listed character references and one party removed from each
> **Education**—opinions of former teachers, school records
> **Neighborhood inquiry**—opinions of present and former neighbors
> **National agency check**—inquiry all national agencies and all local police agencies where the candidate has resided
> **Foreign travel and connections**—when, where, what, why
> **Credit ratings**—past and present
> **Criminal records**—
> **Citizenship of candidate and spouse**—
> **Hobbies**—How does he utilize his free time
> **Assessment of loyalty, integrity, and discretion**—

In addition to the aforementioned items of a typical background investigation, whenever possible, the selection process should include psychiatric screening by a psychiatrist who specializes in the pre-employment selection of police personnel. This certainly does not mean that officers who have demonstrated years of competent police service should have to undergo psychiatric screening before assignment to the intelligence unit. It does imply that those agencies that use this practice at the entrance level do have additional advantages. There are some that disagree with the above point of view.

ORGANIZATION

Maier and Hayes in their text *Creative Management* relate, "What is organization and what is not? The structural framework of organization is people. People, rather than a single person, create the end product of service and carry out the goals through concerted effort. The reason several or many people are involved is self-evident; creating and achieving certain kinds of goals or services is a more extensive task than any single person can undertake alone. The distinctive characteristic of an organization is as simple as that."

As reflected in *Municipal Police Administration*, published by the International Association of City Managers, we find that, "A police force is organized for the purpose of facilitating the attainment of its objectives. Organization is the arrangement of persons with a common purpose in a manner to enable the performance by specific individuals of related tasks grouped for the purpose of assignment, and the establishment of areas of responsibility with clear-cut channels of communication and authority." The intelligence unit is organized for the same purpose as any other group, to promote efficiency.

The principle factors to be considered are division of the work load, chain of command, establishing line of authority and responsibility, unity of command, limits of supervision, and coordination. All of these factors have a direct bearing on the police operational intelligence unit. Each factor comes into greater or lesser significance and all are interrelated.

The moment two or more people are assigned to the intelligence unit, the division of the work load becomes a consideration and enlarges with each new manpower addition. Generally speaking, that area of greatest immediate importance to the intelligence function will receive the largest allocation of manpower. Preparation of current dossiers on personalities involved in local organized crime is one such area that requires a large outlay of man-hours.

The chain of command is the conduit through which flows communication from superiors and subordinates. The traditional theory is that commands flow downward and information flows upward and that they do not skip levels of authority. Chain of command in most police organizations and the paramilitary groups is quite vigorously adhered to; however, in the intelligence service we can observe many of the recently established principles of democratic industrial management entering into the picture. The authoritarian point of view is slowly yielding, particularly in those police agencies that are alert for the opportunities and benefits conferred by such other methods. *There is no contract, law or practical way for ordering up human loyalty, initiative, and enthusiasm.* The number of policemen who have entered college-degree programs has increased tremendously in the last several decades. Their exposure to research regarding employee incentives, motivations, and drives has accelerated the application of modern industrial management method to the police management field. It appears that this trend will continue, slowly modifying the rigid militaristic concepts of command in law enforcement.

A great many of all the police activities, intelligence included, require that each man must have a partner. Safety is certainly not the only consideration; in fact, it is one of the lesser values. The specialization of the tasks within the intelligence units lends itself to the pair or team approach. If one is sick, on vacation, or unavailable, there is still a specialist. The relationship between the degree of exclusive specialization and supplementary specialization will vary with the problem, man-power availability, and prevailing staff attitudes. The maintenance of highly technical routine credit checks will require much less if any. Organizational grouping concepts must remain relatively flexible even though a large part of the task of gathering information requires exclusive specialization. One specialized team may service numerous routine information gathering units, e.g., a team specializing in the installation of clandestine listening devices can service the demands of several other units.

The organizational picture of intelligence operations usually involves two separate divisions, one of administration and one of operations. The administrative division is concerned principally with typical staff activities similar to any other organization. The operations division embraces the line aspect of the tasks. The administrative unit of the department's intelligence family would normally be directed by the assistant commander, whereas line operations more often involve the commander himself.

The assistant commander is often the person responsible for administrative coordination, freeing the commander for planning and operational considerations. Such items as equipment, payroll, vacations, sick leave, routine assignments, training, visitor control, records, and the like can be severely limiting factors if the commander must perform these personally. For this reason and others, the organizational design must make a clear delineation of this group of non-line activities. (See Fig. 10.1 for organization of Los Angeles Police Department's Intelligence Unit.)

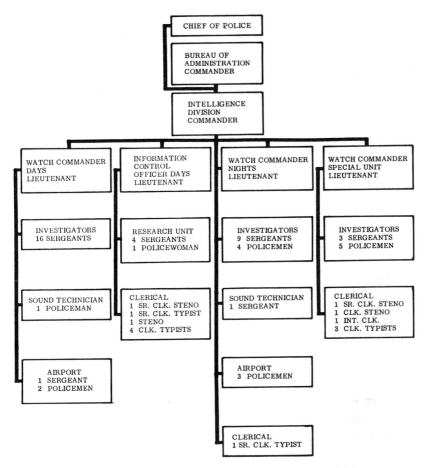

FIGURE 10.1. Table of Organization, Intelligence Division, Los Angeles Police Department, 1966.

Directing the Intelligence Unit

Rigid adherence to authoritarian views on subordinate and superior relationships are not often found in a close working intelligence family. The interactions between policemen and sergeants and between sergeants and lieutenants that are found in a typical line unit such as the patrol division are not apparent in most intelligence organizations. Direction by command is giving way to the idea that police personnel *who participate in decision-making are more cooperative, better informed, and have greater initiative.*

This does not mean that there is a complete disregard and breakdown of rank and authority and every decision is reduced to debate and conference. It does mean that there is and must be a much more relaxed atmosphere regarding status and departmental rank.

In many cases, the unit commander will function as a member of the group, which is a sharp break from traditional police thinking. Acceptance of the unit commander's influence will depend on how he exercises his power and authority. His authority to command is based on the status of his rank; his power is based on his capacity to influence others. Other essentials are job competence and the consideration of the abilities, rights, and human dignity of others. The selection of the unit commander by the chief must give careful consideration to these factors. The potential commander's investigative abilities cannot be neglected either.

A friendly businesslike atmosphere, encompassing shared decision making, coupled with opportunities of a well-founded career service organization, is an ideal philosophy for directing intelligence unit activities. Regularly scheduled conferences which encourage participation by all members of the intelligence team are excellent methods of giving direction and stimulus to operational objectives. These conferences, of course, must be of a democratic nature, not a psuedo-democratic subtle imposition of somebody's will or whim.

Probably the most common form of directing intelligence personnel is through the reporting system. A current inventory of reports pertaining to staff requests is vital to the intelligence product. The unit commander or his assistant acting as the administrative section head, should be constantly aware of pending reports and lagging areas of activity. There must almost be a daily assessment of this picture. The fact that the intelligence product must precede the staff decision makes this direction paramount.

A daily assignment log or a daily resume, regardless of form, will give aid in the direction of the unit. This compilation provides a ready source for the preparation of the weekly briefing that may be required by the chief of police. Security may dictate the form that this assignment log may take. Highly sensitive areas can easily be abbreviated and coded. This log or resume is probably one of the most important administrative devices of the intelligence unit. The ground rules and expectations regarding its use and application must be clearly understood by all unit personnel.

Some large agencies may decentralize the above mentioned log by requiring each team to keep and or submit it daily regarding their current activities. These daily recapitulations are then integrated into a resume and thereafter filed by subject matter activities, personality dossiers, or organizational categories. There may be occasions or tasks the nature of which dictate some other form of direction. Direction of these activities may be limited to regular or intermittent verbal reports. This direction still involves reporting.

If the unit reaches a size that span of control becomes a genuine problem, then the grouping of teams into sections may be advisable. Section leaders or group leaders may be involved in the direction and assignment of four or five teams. However, a highly centralized task assignment is preferable. Centralized general supervision is of less immediate concern to the commander. The focus of the intelligence effort takes on greater importance than the task of supervision. To be overly concerned with supervisory tasks at the expense of the intelligence product is defeating. Men in the intelligence unit must be the type that require *little direct supervision* and only occasional refocusing of effort.

Planning

There is a close similarity between the dimensions labeled "organizing" and "planning." An organizer breaks down jobs into their various tasks, assigns people to perform the tasks, lays out the work, fixes responsibility and follows up to see that things get done; but, in order to do so he must also plan and schedule work and its progress.

Planning must take into account that each officer, who knows what's expected of him, requires less supervision and supervisors must also take into account that if an officer knows how he stands and what is expected of him, this in itself will bring about the invention of informal working patterns which are in harmony with written policy.

Likert in explaining the two central ideas of his "modified theory" of production planning and measurement relates that "the pattern of interaction between the superior and his subordinates *should be supportive rather than threatening*"; and secondly "management can make full use of its human policies only when each employee is a member of a well knit and effectively functioning work group with high interaction skills and performance goals."

Probably the most important planning concept for police intelligence operations is to get as many intelligence personnel as possible involved in the planning phases of an endeavor, with due regard to security measures. The act of participation in planning increases the officers sense of responsiblity to accomplish that which he helped to plan.

Intelligence planning must also be keenly aware of the fundamental differences between the formal organizational structure of the agency and the informal structure. The relationships that are supposed to exist as reflected on a formal organizational chart may not in fact represent the path of communications which contain vital intelligence planning data. Intelligence planning must take this into account.

Every planning task is preceded by a fact-finding phase. This fact-finding phase in police intelligence operations must always include consideration of items of current major staff concern, coupled with the chief's general allocation of relative importance to the overall department objectives. Failure to take this realistically into account in planning intelligence operations can often lead to unnecessary frictions or conflicts.

As a general guide to the concept of police intelligence planning, it can be stated that any organization operates best with a concentration on a limited number of activities. They become less effective each time they add a new function, but, not necessarily less effective when they develop a new target area of interest.

There must be a general understanding of the combined capabilities of the personnel within the intelligence unit. An objective over evaluation of the capability of the intelligence organization will grossly alter the quality of the final product. Planning must include a realistic assessment of just what the unit can and cannot accomplish. The accomplishment of the unit is certainly related to number of personnel assigned and their capacities, funds available, staff attitudes and cooperation, and the length of time that the unit has been in existence.

The defining of the problems or objectives is an integral part of the initial phases of intelligence planning. This serves to focus interest and energy along lines that have greater importance to the department. Misdirected efforts are thus avoided. This early definition of the problem gives a framework for later considerations.

The aims or goals, subject to later modification, should be reduced to a concise statement, free of ambiguity and available to all personnel assigned. The contents of this statement of goals or aims should be mandatory reading and thoroughly understood by each member of the unit. Their future conduct and activities must always operate within the framework of this statement.

An example of such a statement is as follows: "The mission of the intelligence unit is to gather, process, and reduce to usable form information concerning people and things which are inimical to the department and its objectives."

The principal function of the intelligence unit is simply to gather and process information. Planning the activities centers around methods or techniques regarding how to perform this gathering, when and where to do it, and who should do it.

Methods and techniques include, but are not limited to, such things as liaison programs, both internal and external, informant networks, clipping services and de-briefing programs. The planning of these items must be formalized with specific responsibilities assigned.

Financing

Consideration of all things within the intelligence unit could be labeled planning; however, certain administrative aspects are considered separately for convenience. Such things as salary, overtime, per diem, travel, tuitions, confidential funds, maintenance costs, and the like, if not considered in advance, can cripple effective intelligence activities.

Most police agencies utilize line item budgets or in rare cases, program budgets. Within each department it is a typical procedure to have each unit or division commander prepare a budget request each year. Though not a good practice each commander, more often than is wise, waits until a rather late date before commencing this important task.

This delay takes on greater proportions in the intelligence unit and should carefully be avoided. The fact that this occurs is typically exemplified by the usual departmental confusion as the department budget approaches the due date. One method to use to avoid this is to integrate funding into weekly or biweekly intelligence conferences. Another method to further safeguard against budget deficiencies is to issue a small budget notebook to each supervisor or if necessary to each officer. If it is wallet size and its contents are strictly limited to budget items, only a good product can be realized. This permits the immediate recording of needs, not leaving them to individual memory or recall.

The preparation of the intelligence unit budget will vary according to city and department requirements. Generally, a typical intelligence unit budget will include a statement of its objectives or mission, a chart of organizational structure, a list of the general activities performed by each sub-organization unit, and a general description of each activity and how it relates in achieving the overall objectives of the department.

The International Association of City Managers' text *Municipal Finance Administration* states that specific data concerning budgets may typically include the following:

a. A general description of each activity including a statement of objectives in terms of the end result sought.
b. Legal authority for performing the activity
c. Necessity for the activity and what happens if not performed
d. List of sub-activities and operations included in the activity
e. Time factors in performance, when possible and practical
f. Schedule of personnel assigned quoted by man-year and classification
g. Description or listing of facilities used or maintained
h. Equipment and major tools used, by location, number and type
i. List and samples of any printed forms used and copies of monthly, annual, or other periodic reports concerning the activity
j. List factors which influence work load
k. List of statistical units now recorded on work performed and on results achieved and compilation of comparative data for significant number of prior years
l. Comparative cost data showing current and past records of expenditures incurred in carrying on the program if such information can be obtained from accounting records or by analysis.

One danger inherent in cyclical budgeting is that it can invite shortrun thinking and a tendency to postpone necessary expenditure increases to some future budget. Failure to look beyond the current budget can multiply future problems. Intelligence commanders must consider additional personnel increases, and their needs, on a long-range basis as well as on immediate needs. They must also bear in mind that needs for additional personnel proceed at a much faster rate than population increases. This is because the rapid influx of people without roots or, in the case of many, an understanding of how to adapt successfully to the complex problems of city life.

All old established organizations build up a system of values, beliefs, and traditions that change only slowly. The budget for any current cycle is inevitably affected by past commitments, established standards of service, existing organization structure, and current methods of operating, any or all of which may not be entirely satisfactory. The commander must always remember that budgeting should be a continuing process and therefore plan his campaign for the long pull. He should not be too concerned if all his objectives are not achieved in any single budget.

One of the most important aspects of financing police intelligence operations is the "operational fund," that money immediately available for use. It is fair to say that in the intelligence concept, information is a commodity as valuable as gold. The purchase of information is a troublesome decision for many police administrators. Yet, if the purchase of information will save the community thosands of dollars in man-hour expenditures or help prevent the victimizing of its citizens, why not make the purchase? Fairly rigid controls and clear-cut procedures will prevent the abuses that can be alluded to. The principal factor involved is the acceptance of responsibility by supervisors in the intelligence unit.

Practices involving informant payment must always include a receipt system. Administratively it appears wise to strictly limit the power to disburse these funds. Monthly accounting and regeneration of the fund may be more desirable than longer periods.

An expense fund for intelligence personnel assigned to field duties is absolutely imperative. Each officer knows that dedication is admirable but it will not buy things for his wife and family. If the expense fund does not exist, it then requires the officer to reach into his earnings for his family, thus restricting almost all activity involving the spending of money. By way of example, a typical intelligence officer will spend in excess of fifteen dollars a month using public telephones from the field, not to mention other larger expenditures.

There are several methods available for handling the disbursement of these funds. One method is a blanket amount added to each officer's monthly or semi-monthly payroll check. Another involves the submission of monthly detailed vouchers, with case numbers, to recover money already spent by the individual officer. A third could be a monthly cash advance to each officer with quarterly or bimonthly detailed written accounting.

Regardless of the system used to handle expense funds and other confidential funds, quality of production is related to their availability and use. Failure to make these funds available and reasonably usable will determine, in great part, the success or failure of the entire intelligence unit, and perhaps the entire intelligence community. As Dale Carnegie once stated "You usually get just what you pay for."

With the exception of those items previously discussed, the vast majority of financing and budgeting for the intelligence unit can be appropriately handled by the budget division of the department and by city finance. On occasion it may be operationally convenient to have methods available to put special employees on the payroll; however, this is a rare exception.

With a final word on the payment of informants, undercover operators, or whatever name is used, it can be summarized very briefly. There is a certain type of information that only money can economically acquire. When the possession of this information is essential to the police protection of the community, buy it! But, remember, you must be prepared at all times to justify the expenditure.

Intelligence Records

Experience has demonstrated that certain responsibilities are generally appropriate for the records division. Complaint, arrest, identification, and property-control records must be kept completely and accurately; they must be used in identifying persons and property and in providing supervision over investigating officers; the information they contain must be tabulated, summarized, analyzed, and compared in order to measure accomplishments, detect weaknesses, and plan operations. These clearly should be records-division duties.

O. W. Wilson, in his text *Police Administration*, states, "The records division is usually the unit best suited to handle such activities as the booking of prisoners, the maintenance of criminal identification records, the custody and control of property, and the reproduction of records forms, police reports, and publications. In addition, the records division is responsible for a staff supervision of the performance of records tasks and related operations by the members of other divisions.

"From the discussion up to this point, it can readily be seen that the records division should be a central service agency, whose head reports directly to the chief or to his assistant. The records division has no primary police functions but only provides auxiliary services to facilitate the work of the operating divisions and to assist the chief in his job of management. The modern records division performs the work that in the past has been performed by the bureau of identification, the desk sergeant, the booking officer, the communications unit, the property clerk's office, and sometimes the accounting office."

It is apparent from the above that a typical records division performs an intelligence service. The intelligence unit has several general groupings that are almost independent records systems completely divorced from each other and from the central records division. These intelligence records groupings are generally divided into operations and administration, much the same manner in which the unit itself is divided.

The operations records may include a personality file wherein each person is referenced to every report that contains his name. A dossier file on prominent hoodlums should be maintained religiously. In addition, operations records include a vehicle file, telephone number file, and an operation file. Some intelligence units in certain areas may develop other specialized operations files. Operations files may be physically divided into different security levels. Information of a highly sensitive nature may be given additional security by isolating it from daily operational files.

The administrative records will include such items as officers service jackets, including performance activities, payroll, sick leave, attendance, training, vacations, and other similar records may also be kept by the administrative section of the unit. Access to these records is limited just as appropriately as access to operational records; however, it can be generally stated that the majority of administrative records are property of the department of police. Operational records are maintained as property of the chief of police to give added security by preventing them from being subjected to subpoena as provided for by law in most states. An example of this is found in the California Civil Code of Procedure, Section 1886.

Security

Security is everybody's responsibility; however, habits and routines usually become lax if on occasion something is not done to stimulate personnel. The task of developing a "security consciousness" should commence the moment a man enters a law enforcement career. However, it is generally neglected in most recruit academy programs, and the neglect continues throughout the officer's career in almost all agencies.

For discussion purposes, security can be conveniently divided into the following areas: premises, documents, communications, and personnel. However, even with the most elaborate set of security measures, the first and foremost aspect of any security program is the degree of security consciousness of personnel within the agency. Responsibility for security is particularly incumbent upon supervisors and administrators and like any other responsibility it can never be shed.

Certain precautions can be taken which will give added security to any type of structure. Simple locking of doors and windows that should be locked is probably one of the most essential aspects of structural security. Periodic changing of the locks is an added feature which strengthens security. Within the structure, the habitual and mandatory locking of desks, file cabinets, and safes, regardless of content, further adds to the development of security consciousness. Periodic changing of file cabinet locks and safe combinations is desirable. Within the structure, areas that contain particularly sensitive material can be restricted to a limited number of carefully screened personnel. A visitors log and badge control requirements can further refine this. Because of the sensitive nature of certain intelligence operations, security takes on greater importance.

Security of documents involves again the development of a strong group concern for security. Intelligence documents can be classified according to content with limiting access at each level of classification. In addition to the numbering of the documents, an inventory process can be established which will reflect a history of all those who have had the document in their possession. Simple to complex methods can be established for document destruction. These methods can include burning, shredding, and other forms of complete mutilation. If necessary, the contents of highly critical documents can be reduced to a code, though very rarely would this ever be necessary in modern day American police systems.

Modern police agencies use a radio code principally for the conservation of valuable air time. A separate radio frequency for intelligence activities not only adds to this conservation, it also provides an additional element of security. Yet, with this, probably the most valuable asset to communications security is an auxiliary communications system outside of the normal intelligence frequency. Most large police agencies have limited communications security. Intelligence personnel should be constantly reminded that radio monitoring of virtually any frequency is an inexpensive task and available to many whose interests may be alien to the unit and the department.

Training

Training is, without elaboration, a command function. The discredit for existing deficiences involving tool and technique applications falls nowhere except upon "supervision." The first prerequisite of an intelligence supervisor is little different than any other; he must know his job and be able to teach it.

Indoctrination in the value of personal contacts and team effort is near the core of the initial phase of the journey each officer will take before becoming a seasoned intelligence contributor. Stresses placed on tradition for accuracy and *esprit de corps* also provide a valuable training foundation upon which other learning must be based.

In selecting the most fundamental tools that an intelligence officer should have high proficiency in, careful consideration should be given to basic report writing, interrogation, and informant recruitment and development. Most intelligence units have definite formats for report writing. Instruction and mastery require some deviation from typical police reporting. Interrogation ability in the result of much experience and training. Informal interrogation (acquiring information without the knowledge of the subject) requires even more. Informant recruitment and development is an art that is achieved only through the most intensive instruction and practice. It must be completely mastered.

For the new assignee, many techniques of imparting knowledge can be applied. Such methods as lectures, conferences, and tutoring by specialists are available. The most common form of instruction, however, is probably the coach-pupil system. Before being assigned to a seasoned officer, the beginner will have to receive instructions on policies, procedures, facilities, records, and what is expected of him from his supervisors. Almost all personnel, before being assigned to intelligence duties, have acquired extensive police experience in operating line units. Eradication of some bad habits may also be part of the training.

During the course of their career, intelligence officers will migrate to some specialized area. Prior to this migration, it is perhaps well to sufficiently vary their initial assignments to broaden perspective and appreciation. It also better prepares them for supervision.

In order to insure that the training program is established, the intelligence unit commander must assign the responsibility to a specific individual within his command. The selection of this individual must be consistent with his interest and qualifications to perform this valuable staff function.

The training supervisor must develop an in-service training program which is truly comprehensive in meeting the needs of the unit. For example, if the need is established that informant recruitment and development is lagging, then training keyed to this effort will reinforce the supervisory process. Clearly training is essential to fill operational gaps that will occur.

CHAPTER ELEVEN

SUMMARY OF TEXT

The history of police and military intelligence provides some interesting insights, for it appears that only rarely does an untried intelligence concept come along. The artful employers of intelligence agents have been legion. Historians, in their "great-man" treatment of history have somewhat neglected the commanders of the secret, invisible army of intelligence agents which have had a profound effect on the course of events.

Historically speaking, municipal police intelligence services are still in infancy compared to military experience. Examination of the history of law enforcement offers little in regard to the formalization of one of its components, police operational intelligence.

The year 1940 probably marks the beginning of a partially organized intelligence service within law enforcement. The Federal Bureau of Investigation was assigned the responsibility for intelligence gathering in Central and South America. The development of an "intelligence consciousness" among lawmen spread rapidly as a result of the impetus given by J. Edgar Hoover's training schools for intelligence activity.

On March 29, 1955, a group of law enforcement officers representing twenty-six police and sheriff departments from seven states, met in San Francisco, California. The need for some means or organization in law enforcement to exchange confidential information on certain individuals and organizations as well as a central clearing house for this information was outlined. The name committee submitted "Law Enforcement Intelligence Unit" (LEIU) and needless to say, the name was adopted. From this time forward, the Law Enforcement Intelligence Unit became a family of dedicated highly skilled professionals, constantly seeking tenacles of the "Organization."

Police operational intelligence has probably made more

advances in the last twenty years than it did in the previous century. Though an embryo service, the future appears exceptionally bright, full of vast unexplored areas for research and development not yet unveiled.

The aim of the police intelligence unit is to supply the chief of police or his authorized representative with complete and accurate information. If having this will not automatically produce a decision for the executive, it at least may increase the probability of the correct decision. This increase in probability may many times be the difference between success or failure.

Intelligence information which is primarily long-range in nature with little practical immediate operational value can be classified as *strategic intelligence.* The types of intelligence activity which deal with the defending of the agency against its criminal enemies can be appropriately classified as *counter-intelligence.* That type of intelligence which is of an immediate nature and necessary for more effective police planning and operations can be logically classified as *line intelligence.*

Line and strategic intelligence, in most cases, are the result of gathering information from overt sources rather than from hidden confidential informants and the like. Credit bureaus, newspapers (clipping services), transportation and communications media, plus others, form the bulk of strategic intelligence sources and the majority of line intelligence as well. However, we must concede that on many occasions, the most valuable information comes from an underworld informant. This type of highly valuable information more often than not deals with a specific crime, though on occasion it is concerned with gang operations and essential to major police planning.

Some chiefs of police are oblivious to the symptoms of the spreading influence and danger of the "syndicate." To arrest low-level vice violators has little effect on the "organization" for these pawns are easily replaced. Too often, people of the organization are stereotyped as muscle and guns, whereas we know that this is not the new image. Contributing to charities, taking an active part in the church and community youth groups, not excluding the chamber of commerce and the uptown business organizations, are all part of the disarming and powerful mask being adopted by organized crime.

Many misunderstandings exist in the minds of different police administrators regarding what intelligence really is. Police operational intelligence is simply the gathering and processing of information. It is not a magic formula that will resolve all the problems that may be encountered by the police administrator. Intelligence can and should do nothing more than provide the responsible authority with a better understanding of the true picture facing him. It must always be born in mind that intelligence is not a direct action agency, and should never be interpreted as such; its net worth should not be judged by the traditional thinking of the number of arrests performed.

Too often police administrators are required to make major decisions based upon inadequate information. Intelligence must fill the void often existing in police decision-making. *Fundamentally stated, the purpose of the intelligence unit is to increase the probability of accuracy in operational staff decisions.*

With the computerization of police record systems, the time is rapidly approaching when police administrators will be able to perform intricate intelligence functions which will be measured in seconds or fractions of seconds. Predictions of far-reaching magnitude will be the result of the sophistication and application of industrial methods and techniques.

Business transactions of management level criminals will be integrated, analyzed and processed within hours rather than months. Today this is almost an impossibility, yet with current development of the National Crime Information Center, we are rapidly approaching this capability. Data processing for a giant intelligence complex takes on proportions that are difficult to comprehend, in fact, difficult to imagine.

Police intelligence operations involve a number of different tasks, namely discovery and identification activity, surveillance, liaison programs, informant recruitment, clipping services, debriefings, and other miscellaneous activities. These different tasks are part of the actions that go into the preparation of the total intelligence product.

The identification and surveillance of individuals involved in organized crime and subversive activities consumes a considerable part of the police operational intelligence field activities. The identification of the associates and relatives of organized crime personalities is vital to the final intelligence product. It is oftentimes the answer to the question "who owns who" in the community.

Informant recruitment and development ranks very high in mandatory achievements of an intelligence officer. There are definite types of information that can be acquired by no other manner than through the use of informants. The total effectiveness of an intelligence unit can be fairly accurately evaluated at any given time by assessing the number and quality of informants that can be brought to bear in an instant case.

Technical surveillance, electronic surveillance, wire tapping, bugging, call it what you like. It is legal in some jurisdictions and illegal in others. It is employed by some and not by others. One thing is certain, those police agencies that use it are in a much better position to protect the citizens of their respective communities. Its use should be restricted to targets that have a high probability of a good return rather than random selection of doubtfuls.

Total capability of the intelligence unit and priority are the two principal considerations in the selection of intelligence objectives. The outcome of any intelligence endeavor is usually related to the number of personnel available and to their combined and separate abilities. All staff requests must take this into account. Staff priority requests must be realistic with respect to the unit workload at any given time. What would be too great a burden at one moment may not be at another.

Some important considerations in establishing the size of the intelligence unit include overall size of the agency, metropolitan aspects, and the estimated infiltration of organized crime and other related aspects. Unfortunately, this latter category is difficult to evaluate without the unit being in existence. After the intelligence unit is formalized, organized crime comes under greater scrutiny; an expansion of coverage is not necessarily a demonstration of Parkinson's Law in action.

Selection of the intelligence division commander by the chief of police is probably one of the most important tasks to be performed. Coupled with other attributes, loyalty is paramount, however, loyalty should never be confused with blind obedience. The two are grossly different. Though the chief will never find one with all the traits he is seeking, prime consideration should be given to that staff member who is not a "yes" man. He must be a person who consistently acts to provide truth, unshadowed, and in its simplest form regardless of personalities involved.

The organizational picture of intelligence operations usually involves two separate divisions, one of administration and one of operations. The administrative division is concerned principally with typical staff activities similar to any other organization. The operations division embraces the line aspect of the tasks. The administrative unit of the department's intelligence family would normally be directed by the assistant commander, whereas line operations more often involve the commander himself. The assistant commander is often the person responsible for administrative coordination, freeing the commander for planning and operational considerations.

In many cases, the unit commander will function as a member of the group, which is a sharp break from traditional police thinking. Acceptance of the unit commander's influence will depend on how he exercises his power and authority. His authority to command is based on the status of his rank; his power is based on his capacity to influence others.

GUIDE TO SUBVERSIVE ORGANIZATIONS

Name of Organization and Date of Designation Under Executive Order 10450:

Abraham Lincoln Brigade, April 29, 1953.

Abraham Lincoln School, Chicago, Illinois, April 29, 1953.

Action Committee To Free Spain Now, April 29, 1953.

Alabama People's Educational Association (see Communist Political Association).

American Association for Reconstruction in Yugoslavia, Inc., April 29, 1953.

American Branch of the Federation of Greek Maritime Unions, April 29, 1953.

American Christian Nationalist Party, April 29, 1953.

American Committee for European Workers' Relief (see Socialist Workers Party).

American Commitee for Protection of Foreign Born, April 29, 1953.

American Committee for Spanish Freedom, April 29, 1953.

American Committee for the Settlement of Jews in Birobidjan, Inc., September 28, 1953.

American Committee for Yugoslav Relief, Inc., April 29, 1953.

American Committee To Survey Labor Conditions in Europe, July 15, 1953.

American Council for a Democratic Greece (formerly known as the Greek American Council; Greek American Committee for National Unity), April 29, 1953.

American Council on Soviet Relations, April 29, 1953.

American Croatian Congress, April 29, 1953.

American Jewish Labor Council, April 29, 1953.

American League Against War and Fascism, April 29, 1953.

American League for Peace and Democracy, April 29, 1953.

American National Labor Party, April 29, 1953.

American National Socialist League, April 29, 1953.

American National Socialist Party, April 29, 1953.

American National Party, April 29, 1953.

American Patriots, Inc., April 29, 1953.

American Peace Crusade, January 22, 1954.
American Peace Mobilization, April 29, 1953.
American Poles for Peace, July 15, 1953.
American Polish Labor Council, April 29, 1953.
American Polish League, January 22, 1954.
American Rescue Ship Mission (a project of the United American Spanish Aid Committee), April 29, 1953.
American-Russian Fraternal Society, April 29, 1953.
American Russian Institute, New York (also known as the American Russian Institute for Cultural Relations with the Soviet Union), April 29, 1953.
American Russian Institute, Philadelphia, April 29, 1953.
American Russian Institute of San Francisco, April 29, 1953.
American Russian Institute of Southern California, Los Angeles, April 29, 1953.
American Slav Congress, April 29, 1953.
American Women for Peace, January 22, 1954.
American Youth Congress, April 29, 1953.
American Youth for Democracy, April 29, 1953.
Armenian Progressive League of America, April 29, 1953.
Associated Klans of America, April 29, 1953.
Association of Georgia Klans, April 29, 1953.
Association of German Nationals (Reichsdeutsche Vereinigung), April 29, 1953.
Ausland-Organization der NSDAP, Overseas Branch of Nazi Party, April 29, 1953.
Baltimore Forum, July 15, 1953.
Benjamin Davis Freedom Committee, April 4, 1955.
Black Dragon Society, April 29, 1953.
Boston School for Marxist Studies, Boston, Massachusetts, April 29, 1953.
Bridges-Robertson-Schmidt Defense Committee, July 15, 1953.
Bulgarian American People's League of the United States of America, September 28, 1953.
California Emergency Defense Committee, July 15, 1953.
California Labor School, Inc., 321 Divisadero Street, San Francisco, California, April 29, 1953.
Carpatho-Russian People's Society, April 29, 1953.
Central Council of American Women of Croatian Descent (also known as Central Council of American Croatian Women, National Council of Croatian Women), April 29, 1953.

Central Japanese Association (Beikoku Chuo Nipponjin Kai), April 29, 1953.

Central Japanese Association of Southern California, April 29, 1953.

Central Organization of the German-American National Alliance (Deutsche-Amerikanische Einheitsfront), April 29, 1953.

Cervantes Fraternal Society, April 29, 1953.

China Welfare Appeal, Inc., January 22, 1954.

Chopin Cultural Center, July 15, 1953.

Citizens Committee for Harry Bridges, April 29, 1953.

Citizens Committee of the Upper West Side (New York City), April 29, 1953.

Citizens Committee to Free Earl Browder, April 29, 1953.

Citizens Emergency Defense Conference, January 22, 1954.

Citizens Protective League, April 29, 1953.

Civil Liberties Sponsoring Committee of Pittsburgh, April 4, 1955.

Civil Rights Congress and its affiliated organizations, including: Civil Rights Congress for Texas. Veterans Against Discrimination of Civil Rights Congress of New York, April 29, 1953.

Civil Rights Congress for Texas (see Civil Rights Congress) Columbians, April 29, 1953.

Comite Coordinador Pro Republica Espanola, April 29, 1953.

Comite Pro Derechos Civiles (see Puerto Rican Comite pro Libertades Civiles).

Committee for a Democratic Far Eastern Policy, April 29, 1953.

Committee for Constitutional and Political Freedom, July 15, 1953.

Committee for Nationalist Action, April 29, 1953.

Committee for Peace and Brotherhood Festival in Philadelphia, September 28, 1953.

Committee for the Defense of the Pittsburgh Six, July 15, 1953.

Committee for the Negro in the Arts, January 22, 1954.

Committee for the Protection of the Bill of Rights, September 28, 1953.

Committee for World Youth Friendship and Cultural Exchange, July 15, 1953.

Committee To Abolish Discrimination in Maryland (also known as Congress Against Discrimination; Maryland Congress Against Discrimination; Provisional Committee to Abolish Discrimination in the State of Maryland), April 4, 1955.

Committee to Aid the Fighting South, April 29, 1953.

Committee to Defend Marie Richardson, July 15, 1953.

Committee to Defend the Rights and Freedom of Pittsburgh's Political Prisoners, April 4, 1955.

Committee to Uphold the Bill of Rights, September 28, 1953.
Commonwealth College, Mena, Arkansas, April 29, 1953.
Communist Party, U.S.A., its subdivisions, subsidiaries and affiliates, April 29, 1953.
Communist Political Association, its subdivisions, subsidiaries and affiliates, including:
Alabama People's Educational Association.
Florida Press and Educational League.
Oklahoma League for Political Education.
People's Educational and Press Association of Texas.
Virginia League for People's Education, April 29, 1953.
Congress Against Discrimination (see Committee to Abolish Discrimination in Maryland).
Congress of American Revolutionary Writers, April 29, 1953.
Congress of American Women, April 29, 1953.
Congress of the Unemployed, April 4, 1955.
Connecticut Committee to Aid Victims of the Smith Act, January 22, 1954.
Connecticut State Youth Conference, April 29, 1953.
Council for Jobs, Relief and Housing, July 15, 1953.
Council for Pan-American Democracy, April 29, 1953.
Council of Greek Americans, July 15, 1953.
Council on African Affairs, April 29, 1953.
Croatian Benevolent Fraternity, April 29, 1953.
Dai Nippon Butoku Kai (Military Virtue Society of Japan or Military Art Society of Japan), April 29, 1953.
Daily Worker Press Club, April 29, 1953.
Daniels Defense Committee, January 22, 1954.
Dante Alighieri Society (between 1935 and 1940), April 20, 1953.
Dennis Defense Committee, April 29, 1953.
Detroit Youth Assembly, April 29, 1953.
East Bay Peace Committee, April 4, 1955.
Elsinore Progressive League, October 20, 1955.
Emergency Conference to Save Spanish Refugees (founding body of the North American Spanish Aid Committee), April 29, 1953.
Everybody's Committee to Outlaw War, October 20, 1955.
Families of the Baltimore Smith Act Victims, January 22, 1954.
Families of the Smith Act Victims, January 22, 1954.
Federation of Italian War Veterans in the U.S.A., Inc. (Associatiazone Nationale Combattenti Italiani, Federazione degli Stati Uniti d' America), April 29, 1953.

Finnish-American Mutual Aid Society, April 29, 1953.

Florida Press and Educational League (see Communist Political Association).

Frederick Douglass Education Center, September 28, 1953.

Freedom Stage, Inc., January 22, 1954.

Friends of the New Germany (Freunde des Neusen Deutschlands), April 29, 1953.

Friends of the Soviet Union, April 29, 1953.

Garibaldi American Fraternal Society, April 29, 1953.

George Washington Carver School, New York City, April 29, 1953.

German-American Bund (Amerikadeutscher Volksbund), April 29, 1953.

German-American Republican League, April 29, 1953.

German-American Vocational League (Deutsche-Amerikanische Berufsgemeinschaft), April 29, 1953.

Guardian Club, April 4, 1955.

Harlem Trade Union Council, September 28, 1953.

Hawaii Civil Liberties Committee, April 29, 1953.

Heimusha Kai, also known as Nokubei Heieki Gimusha Kai, Zaibel Nihonjin, Heiyaku Gimusha Kai, and Zaibei Heimusha Kai (Japanese Residing in America Military Conscripts Association), April 29, 1953.

Hellenic-American Brotherhood, April 29, 1953.

Hinode Kai (Imperial Japanese Reservists), April 29, 1953.

Hinomaru Kai (Rising Sun Flag Society—a group of Japanese War Veterans), April 29, 1953.

Hokubei Zaigo Shoke Dan (North American Reserve Officers Association), April 29, 1953.

Hollywood Writers Mobilization for Defense, April 29, 1953.

Hungarian-American Council for Democracy, April 29, 1953.

Hungarian Brotherhood, April 29, 1953.

Idaho Pension Union, October 20, 1955.

Independent Party (Seattle, Washington) (also known as Independent People's Party), April 4, 1955.

Independent People's Party (see Independent Party).

Industrial Workers of the World, April 29, 1953.

International Labor Defense, April 29, 1953.

International Workers Order, its subdivisions, subsidiaries and affiliates, April 29, 1953.

Japanese Association of America, April 29, 1953.

Japanese Overseas Central Society (Kaigai Dobo Chuo Kai), April 29, 1953.

Japanese Overseas Convention, Tokyo, Japan, 1940, April 29, 1953.

Japanese Protective Association (Recruiting Organization), April 29, 1953.

Jefferson School of Social Science, New York City, April 29, 1953.

Jewish Culture Society, July 15, 1953.

Jewish People's Committee, April 29, 1953.

Jewish People's Fraternal Order, April 29, 1953.

Jikyoku Lin Kai (The Committee for the Crisis), April 29, 1953.

Johnson-Forest Group (also known as Johnsonites), April 4, 1955.

Johnsonites (see Johnson-Forest Group).

Joint Anti-Fascist Refugee Committee, April 29, 1953.

Joint Council of Progressive Italian-Americans, Inc., September 28, 1953.

Joseph Weydemeyer School of Social Science, St. Louis, Missouri, April 29, 1953.

Kibei Seinen Kai (Association of U.S. Citizens of Japanese Ancestry who have returned to America after studying in Japan), April 29, 1953.

Knights of the White Camellia, April 29, 1953.

Ku Klux Klan, April 29, 1953.

Kyffhaeuser, also known as Kyffhaeuser League (Kyffhaeuser Bund), Kyffhaeuser Fellowship (Kyffhaeuser Kameradschaft), April 29, 1953.

Kyffhaeuser War Relief (Kyffhaeuser Kriegshilfswerk), April 29, 1953.

Labor Council for Negro Rights, September 28, 1953.

Labor Research Association, Inc., April 29, 1953.

Labor Youth League, April 29, 1953.

League for Common Sense, April 4, 1955.

League of American Writers, April 29, 1953.

Lictor Society (Italian Black Shirts), April 29, 1953.

Macedonian-American People's League, April 29, 1953.

Mario Morgantini Circle, April 29, 1953.

Maritime Labor Committee to Defend Al Lannon, September 28, 1953.

Maryland Congress Against Discrimination (see Committee to Abolish Discrimination in Maryland).

Massachusetts Committee for the Bill of Rights, October 20, 1955.

Massachusetts Minute Women for Peace (not connected with the Minute Women of the U.S.A., Inc.), January 22, 1954.

Maurice Braverman Defense Committee, July 15, 1953.

Michigan Civil Rights Federation, April 29, 1953.
Michigan Council for Peace, April 4, 1955.
Michigan School of Social Science, April 29, 1953.
Nanka Teikoku Gunyudan (Imperial Military Friends Group or Southern California War Veterans), April 29, 1953.
National Association of Mexican Americans (also known as Asociacion Nacional Mexico-Americana), January 22, 1954.
National Blue Star Mothers of America (not to be confused with the Blue Star Mothers of America organized in February 1942), April 29, 1953.
National Committee for Freedom of the Press, July 15, 1953.
National Committee for the Defense of Political Prisoners, April 29, 1953.
National Committee to Win Amnesty for Smith Act Victims, April 4, 1955.
National Committee to Win the Peace, April 29, 1953.
National Conference on American Policy in China and the Far East (a Conference called by the Committee for a Democratic Far Eastern Policy), April 29, 1953.
National Council of Americans of Croatian Descent, April 29, 1953.
National Council of American-Soviet Friendship, April 29, 1953.
National Federation for Constitutional Liberties, April 29, 1953.
National Labor Conference for Peace, September 28, 1953.
National Negro Congress, April 29, 1953.
National Negro Labor Council, January 22, 1954.
Nationalist Action League, April 29, 1953.
Nationalist Party of Puerto Rico, July 15, 1953.
Nature Friends of America (since 1935), April 29, 1953.
Negro Labor Victory Committee, April 29, 1953.
New Committee for Publications, April 29, 1953.
Nichibei Kogyo Kaisha (The Great Fujii Theatre), April 29, 1953.
North American Committee to Aid Spanish Democracy, April 29, 1953.
North American Spanish Aid Committee, April 29, 1953.
North Philadelphia Forum, July 15, 1953.
Northwest Japanese Association, April 29, 1953.
Ohio School of Social Sciences, April 29, 1953.
Oklahoma Committee to Defend Political Prisoners, April 29, 1953.
Oklahoma League for Political Education (see Communist Political Association).
Original Southern Klans, Incorporated, April 29, 1953.
Pacific Northwest Labor School, Seattle, Washington, April 29, 1953.

Palo Alto Peace Club, January 22, 1954.
Partido Del Pueblo of Panama (Operating in the Canal Zone), April 29, 1953.
Peace Information Center, September 28, 1953.
Peace Movement of Ethiopia, April 29, 1953.
People's Drama, Inc., September 28, 1953.
People's Educational and Press Association of Texas (see Communist Political Association).
People's Educational Association (incorporated under name Los Angeles Educational Association, Inc), also known as People's Educational Center, People's University, People's School, April 29, 1953.
People's Institute of Applied Religion, April 29, 1953.
People's Programs (Seattle, Washington), April 4, 1955.
People's Radio Foundation, Inc., April 29, 1953.
People's Rights Party, April 4, 1955.
Philadelphia Labor Committee for Negro Rights, September 28, 1953.
Philadelphia School of Social Science and Art, April 29, 1953.
Photo League (New York City), April 29, 1953.
Pittsburgh Arts Club, April 4, 1955.
Political Prisoners' Welfare Committee, July 15, 1953.
Polonia Society of the IWO, April 29, 1953.
Progressive German-Americans, also known as Progressive German-Americans of Chicago, April 29, 1953.
Proletarian Party of America, April 29, 1953.
Protestant War Veterans of the United States, Inc., April 29, 1953.
Provisional Committee of Citizens for Peace, Southwest Area, September 28, 1953.
Provisional Committee on Latin American Affairs, April 4, 1955.
Provisional Committee to Abolish Discrimination in the State of Maryland (see Committee to Abolish Discrimination in Maryland).
Puerto Rican Comite Pro Libertades Civiles (CLC) (also known as Comite Pro Derechos Civiles), April 4, 1955.
Puertorriquenos Unidos (Puerto Ricans United), September 28, 1953.
Quad City Committee for Peace, September 28, 1953.
Queensbridge Tenants League, April 4, 1955.
Revolutionary Workers League, April 29, 1953.
Romanian-American Fraternal Society, April 29, 1953.
Russian American Society, Inc., July 15, 1953.
Sakura Kai (Patriotic Society, or Cherry Association—composed of veterans of Russo-Japanese War), April 29, 1953.
Samuel Adams School, Boston, Massachusetts, April 29, 1953.

Santa Barbara Peace Forum, September 28, 1953.

Schappes Defense Committee, April 29, 1953.

Schneiderman-Darcy Defense Committee, April 29, 1953.

School of Jewish Studies, New York City, April 29, 1953.

Seattle Labor School, Seattle, Washington, April 29, 1953.

Serbian-American Fraternal Society, April 29, 1953.

Serbian Vidovdan Council, April 29, 1953.

Shinto Temples (limited to State Shinto abolished in 1945), April 29, 1953.

Silver Shirt Legion of America, April 29, 1953.

Slavic Council of Southern California, January 22, 1954.

Slovak Workers Society, April 29, 1953.

Slovenian-American National Council, April 29, 1953.

Socialist Workers Party, including American Committee for European Workers' Relief, April 29, 1953.

Sokoku Kai (Fatherland Society), April 29, 1953.

Southern Negro Youth Congress, April 29, 1953.

Suiko Sha (Reserve Officers Association, Los Angeles), April 29, 1953.

Syracuse Women for Peace, April 4, 1955.

Tom Paine School of Social Science, Philadelphia, Pennsylvania, April 29, 1953.

Trade Union Committee for Peace (also known as Trade Unionists for Peace), April 4, 1955.

Trade Unionists for Peace (see Trade Union Committee for Peace).

Tri-State Negro Trade Union Council, September 28, 1953.

Ukrainian-American Fraternal Union, April 29, 1953.

Union of American Croatians, April 29, 1953.

Union of New York Veterans, September 28, 1953.

United American Spanish Aid Committee, April 29, 1953.

United Committee of Jewish Societies and Landsmanschaft Federations, also known as Coordination Committee of Jewish Landsmanschaften and Fraternal Organizations, July 15, 1953.

United Committee of South Slavic Americans, April 29, 1953.

United Defense Council of Southern California, April 4, 1955.

United Harlem Tenants and Consumers Organization, April 29, 1953.

United May Day Committee, April 29, 1953.

United Negro and Allied Veterans of America, April 29, 1953.

Veterans Against Discrimination of Civil Rights Congress of New York (see Civil Rights Congress).

Veterans of the Abraham Lincoln Brigade, April 29, 1953.

Virginia League for People's Education (see Communist Political Association).

Voice of Freedom Committee, September 28, 1953.

Walt Whitman School of Social Science, Newark, New Jersey, April 29, 1953.

Washington Bookshop Association, April 29, 1953.

Washington Committee for Democratic Action, April 29, 1953.

Washington Committee to Defend the Bill of Rights, July 15, 1953.

Washington Commonwealth Federation, April 29, 1953.

Washington Pension Union, January 22, 1954.

Wisconsin Conference on Social Legislation, April 29, 1953.

Workers Alliance (since April 1936), April 29, 1953.

Yiddisher Kultur Farband, April 29, 1953.

Young Communist League, April 29, 1953.

Yugoslav-American Cooperative Home, Inc., September 28, 1953.

Yugoslav Seamen's Club, Inc., January 22, 1954.

SUBVERSIVE ACTIVITIES CONTROL BOARD

The Board

The Subversive Activities Control Board is a quasi-court to hear and decide cases brought before it as parties as specified in the Subversive Activities Control Act. The Board neither conducts investigations nor originates actions.

Organization and Functions

The Board is an independent agency composed of five members appointed by the President and confirmed by the Senate for terms of 5 years. The Chairman of the Board is designated by the President. The Board is assisted by a staff which includes attorneys, clerks, and stenographers.

The Board, on petition of the Attorney General, conducts hearings and determines whether any organization is a "Communist-action organization" or a "Communist-front organization" or a "Communist-infiltrated organization" as those terms are defined in the Subversive Activities Control Act of 1950, as amended, and whether any individual is a member of any Communist-action organization. Any organization or individual once having come within the provisions of the Act may, pursuant to prescribed statutory conditions, file with the Board a petition for appropriate relief.

Following hearings the Board issues written findings of fact (designated as the "Report of the Board") and its findings are accompanied by an appropriate order. Decisions and orders of the Board may be taken by the parties aggrieved to the United States Court of Appeals for the District of Columbia for judicial review and, upon certiorari, to the Supreme Court of the United States. When an appeal is taken the order of the Board does not become final unless affirmed by the courts or the appeal is dismissed by the courts.

All pleadings and other papers in proceedings before the Board may be "filed" by mail addressed to the Board or by delivery in person. Proceedings are governed by the Board's published rules of procedure. The Board maintains a docket giving the chronology of each proceeding. The dockets are available for inspection at the office of the Board.

The office of the Board is located in the Lafayette Building, 811 Vermont Avenue NW., Washington, D.C. 20445. The office is open to the public from 9 a.m. to 5 p.m. Mondays through Fridays with the exception of holidays. The Board does not maintain any field offices. The Board provides a reading room or reading area where records will be made available. In addition, there are available in the public reading room copies of the Subversive Activities Control Act of 1950 and of the various amendments thereof, a copy of Title 50 of the United States Code, and a copy of Title 28 of the Code of Federal Regulations.

Requests, Generally

Requests for inspection or copying of records may be made in person or by mail to the clerk of the Board. Those visiting the Board in person should go to the Reception Room which is appropriately marked. Telephone inquiries or requests may be made by calling Washington, D.C., number 382-6224 (area code 202). Collect calls cannot be accepted. Written requests for information should be addressed to the Clerk, Subversive Activities Control Board at the address given above. Where a request is for materials of which copies are not otherwise available and reproductions must be made or where a search is necessary to locate records, the person making the request must pay the costs thereof in advance. The Board maintains a schedule of current costs for reproductions and record searching, and copies of the schedule may be obtained on request. An additional charge as set forth in the schedule is made for certified copies.

Generally Available Material

Rules of procedure.—The Board's rules of procedure, which govern proceedings before the Board, are published in the Federal Register and in Title 28, Chapter II, of the Code of Federal Regulations. Copies may be obtained from the Board on request. Copies are free to parties and their representatives in proceedings in the Board. A charge as set forth in current schedules is payable by others.

Precedent decisions and rulings.—All final opinions (including concurring and dissenting opinions) and all orders made in the adjudication of cases, and all intermediate or other rulings which may have precedential value are published periodically in bound volumes entitled "Reports of the Subversive Activities Control Board." Volumes I through IV cover the period from the inception of the Board to June 30, 1966. A separate volume entitled "Reports of the SACB Index-Digest, Vols. I-IV" contains digests under appropriate topical headings of all rulings enunciated by the Board in the cases contained in the four volumes of the printed Reports. These volumes and the index-digest may be purchased from the Superintendent of Documents, U.S. Government Printing Office, Washington, D.C. 20402. They may be read at the office of the Board. Opinions, orders, and precedential rulings not yet contained in printed volumes, and a cumulative index, are available for inspection and copying at the Board's office.

The pleadings, transcript of testimony, exhibits, and all other papers received in evidence or made a part of the record in Board proceedings (except material exempted under section 5 U.S.C. 552 (b) and received in camera and sealed) are available at the office of the Board for inspection and copying. Copies of the transcripts of testimony when available from the official reporter must be purchased from the reporter at currently prevailing prices. Copies of other documents of record and of the transcripts of testimony when not available from the official reporter may be obtained as set forth above. Where the Board has filed in a court a certified list of the record in a proceding and the Board has retained the record as custodian for the court, no part of such record will be made available unless the person making the request first obtains the permission of the court for the Board to make such documents available.

Statements of policy, interpretations, manuals, instructions to the staff.—The Board being a quasi-court and not having investigatory or enforcement functions has not made statements of policy or interpretations other than as are contained in the rulings, opinions, and orders covered above, nor has the Board issued any manuals or instructions to the staff that affect the public. If any statements of policy, interpretations, manuals or instructions to the staff that affect the public should be issued subsequent to July 4, 1967, and are not part of the material described above, such will be made available with an accompanying index for inspection and copying at the office of the Board.

Other Records

Identifiable records (other than those previously covered) except as are within the exemptions contained in paragraph (b) of 5 U.S.C. 552

and are determined to be of a nature that must be withheld, will be made available upon request and compliance with the provisions contained herein. Such requests may be made as set forth and must contain a reasonably specific description of the particular record sought. The making available of records which are in use in the Board may be deferred until such records no longer are in use or as necessary to avoid disruption of the Board's activities.

Authority to determine which records shall be made available and which are properly to be withheld is vested in the General Counsel of the Board and his decision shall be final except that any person may appeal a decision whereby a request for identifiable records has been denied. Such appeal shall be in writing, addressed to the Board, and shall describe the records sought. The Board will rule upon such appeal at the earliest practicable date and will promptly notify the complainant of its decision.

JURISDICTION AND AUTHORITY

The Subversive Activities Control Board is established and its general powers and functions defined in sections 12 and 13 of the Subversive Activities Control Act, first enacted as Title I of the Internal Security Act of 1950, 64 Stat. 987. The Act has been amended in substance by the Communist Control Act of 1954, 68 Stat. 775, and by Public Law 90-237.

The statute opens with findings of the existence and nature of "a world Communist movement" and the danger posted by the movement "to the security of the United States and to the existence of free American institutions." In enacting the January 1968 amendments to the statute, the Congress reiterated the findings contained in the original statute and the Congress declared that "Disclosure of Communist organizations and of members of Communist-action organizations as provided in this Act is essential to the protection of the national welfare.

The Act as amended defines and authorizes proceedings in the Board for the disclosure of Communist-action organizations, Communist-front organizations, and Communist-infiltrated organizations. It prohibits certain privileges to such organizations and their members. It provides for the disclosure of all members of Communist-action organizations and imposes additional prohibitions on them. An organization determined to be of a type defined in the Act must so identify its mail and radio and television broadcasts. The 1968 amendment eliminated compulsory registration after an order of the Board becomes final determining an organization to be Communist-action or Communist-front, or an individual to be a member of a Communist-action organization. Provisions were made to prevent undue delays of Board hearings by dilatory litigation in the courts, and to penalize misbehaviour which disrupts the hearings. To assure a full and true disclosure of the facts, immunity may be given for certain types of compelled testimony.

Disclosure and the mandatory provisions of the Act, sometimes called "sanctions," become applicable to organizations and individuals only following proceedings before the Subversive Activities Control Board. Under the Act, whenever the Attorney General of the United States has reason to believe that an organization or an individual comes within the provisions of the Act, he petitions the Board for a hearing and determination of the status of such organization or individual. Provision is made for an organization or individual once finally determined in a proceeding before the Board to come within the Act to petition the Board for a hearing and determination that the organization or individual no longer is of the type described in the Act, and for relief from further application of the Act to the organization or individual.

A full, public hearing with ample procedural safeguards is guaranteed any organization or individual involved in a preceeding before the Board. Each party to a proceeding (the Attorney General and the organization or individual, as the case may be) has the right to present its case with the assistance of counsel, to offer oral or documentary evidence, to submit rebuttal evidence, and to conduct such cross-examination as may be required for a full and true disclosure of the facts. An accurate stenographic record is taken of the testimony of each witness and a transcript filed in the office of the Board. The Board may compel by subpena the attendance and testimony of witnesses and the production of relevant documents.

Hearings in Board proceedings may be conducted by the Board or any member thereof or any examiner designated by the Board. The provisions of the Administrative Procedure Act are applicable to such hearings. When the hearing has been conducted by a member of the Board or by a hearing examiner, the hearing officer issues and serves on the parties a recommended decision, and the parties have the opportunity to submit exceptions and briefs for the consideration of the Board and to argue them orally. The Board's determination takes the form of a decision in writing in which the Board states its findings as to the facts and issues an appropriate order.

The party aggrieved by any order of the Board may obtain review by filing in the U.S. Court of Appeals for the District of Columbia Circuit a petition praying that the order be set aside, with opportunity for review by the Supreme Court upon certiorari. The findings of the Board as to the facts, if supported by the preponderance of the evidence, shall be conclusive. If an appeal is taken, orders of the Board do not become final until affirmed by the appellate courts. When an order of the Board has become final the Board publishes in the Federal Register the fact that the order has become final.

The Act provides for the imposition of criminal penalties upon those who fail to abide by the provisions of the Act which apply when an order of the Board has become final. The enforcement of the various consequences which follow from a final Board order involves separate proceedings depending upon action taken or not taken after the order becomes final, and the Board has no functions or duties in such matters.

PROCEEDINGS UNDER THE ACT

Communist Party Membership Cases

The Act provides that whenever the Attorney General shall have reason to believe that any individual is a member of an organization which has been determined by final order of the Board to be a Communist-action organization, he shall file with the Board a petition for a determination that such individual is a member of such Communist-action organization. The Board's order determining the Communist Party of the United States of America to be a Communist-action organization became final on October 20, 1961. On January 16, 1968, the Board modified said final order to conform to the provisions of section 14 (a) of Public Law 90-237, the Act of January 2, 1968.

For the most part the evidence presented by the Attorney General in membership cases established that the individuals involved had been present at, and had participated in, meetings and other affairs of the Communist Party. Most of the witnesses presented by the Attorney General had themselves been members of the Communist Party serving as informants for the Federal Bureau of Investigation. While the individuals involved were represented by counsel during the course of the evidentiary hearings none of them presented any evidence to rebut or contradict the evidence presented by the Attorney General.

Communist-Front Organization Cases

Throughout fiscal year 1969, there was one active case pending in the Board under the Communist-front provisions of the Act. This case involved the W.E.B. DuBois Clubs of America. Just prior to the beginning of the fiscal year the Board granted an unopposed motion of the Attorney General to continue the scheduled hearings in this case until the Supreme Court decided a case then pending before it which the Attorney General represented had special importance in the field of national security and which he apparently expected would furnish useful guidelines in the DuBois case. The Supreme Court rendered its decision in this case (Alderman v. United States, 394 U.S. 165) on March 10, 1969. As of the close of the fiscal year the evidentiary hearings in the DuBois Clubs case had not begun.

Four other cases involving the Communist-front provisions of the Act were being held in the status of indefinite abeyance throughout fiscal year 1969, pursuant to guidelines laid down by the U.S. Court of Appeals for the District of Columbia Circuit. The inactive cases involve organizations which had ceased activities when faced with final orders bringing them within the Communist-front provisions of the Act. If the organizations reactivate the Board may reopen the records and conduct such further proceedings as are appropriate. The organizations involved are:

ADVANCE, AN ORGANIZATION OF PROGRESSIVE YOUTH
AMERICAN PEACE CRUSADE
COLORADO COMMITTEE TO PROTECT CIVIL LIBERTIES
LABOR YOUTH LEAGUE

BIBLIOGRAPHY

Books

1. *Administrative Organization.* John M. Pfiffner and Frank P. Sherwood, Prentice-Hall Inc., Englewood Cliffs, New Jersey, 1960.
2. *Automatic Data Processing.* Elias M. Awad, Prentice-Hall Inc., Englewood Cliffs, New Jersey, 1966.
3. *Automatic Data-Processing Systems.* R. H. Gregory & R. C. VanHorn, Wadsworth Publishing Company, Inc., 1960.
4. *Brotherhood of Evil-The Mafia.* Frederic Sondern Jr., Farrar, Straus, and Cudahy, New York, 1959.
5. *Can American Democracy Survive Cold War.* Harry Howe Ransom, Doubleday & Company, Inc., Garden City, New York, 1963.
6. *Central-Intelligence and National Security.* Harry Howe Ransom, Harvard University Press, Cambridge, Massachusetts, 1959.
7. *Computers and Automation.* Industrial Securities Committee, Berkeley Enterprises Inc., 1962.
8. *Counter Revolution.* James H. Heisel, Atherton Press, New York, 1966.
9. *The Communist Attack on U.S. Police.* W. Cleon Skousen, The Ensign Publishing Company, Salt Lake City, Utah, 1966.
10. *Creative Management.* Norman R. F. Maier and John J. Hayes, John Wiley & Sons Inc., New York-London, 1962.
11. *Crime Detection.* B. Dalton O'Sullivan, The O'Sullivan Publishing House, Chicago, Illinois, 1928.
12. *The Crime Laboratory.* Paul L. Kirk and Lowell W. Bradford, Charles C. Thomas, Publisher, Springfield, Illinois, 1965.
13. *The Death of James Forrestal.* Cornell Simpson, Western Islands, Boston, Los Angeles, 1966.
14. *Digital Computer Primer.* E. M. McCormock, McGraw-Hill Book Co., New York, Toronto, & London, 1959.
15. *Drug Addiction.* David P. Ausubell, Random House, New York, 1958.
16. *Electronic Data Processing.* Wainright Martin Jr., Richard D. Irwin Inc., Homewood, Illinois, 1965.
17. *The Electronic Invasion.* Robert M. Brown, John F. Rider Inc., New York, 1967.
18. *The Fine Art of Spying.* Walter B. Gibson, Crossett and Dunlap, New York, 1965.

19. *High-Speed Data Processing.* C. C. Gotlieb and J. N. P. Hume, McGraw-Hill Book Co., New York, Toronto, & London, 1958.
20. *THE HOLY BIBLE,* The King James Version.
21. *The Informer in Law Enforcement.* Malachi L. Harvey and John C. Cross, Charles C. Thomas, Publisher, Springfield, Illinois, 1962.
22. *Interrogation for Investigators.* Richard O. Arther and Rudolph R. Caputo, William C. Copp & Associates, New York, 1959.
23. *Introduction to Probability and Statistics.* 3rd Edition, Henry Alder and Edward B. Roessler, W. H. Freeman and Co., San Francisco & London, 1964.
24. *Masters of Deceit.* J. Edgar Hoover, Cardinal Edition Pocket Books Inc., New York, 1961.
25. *Microfilm in Business.* Joseph L. Kish Jr. and James Morris, The Ronald Press Co., New York, 1966.
26. *Modern Criminal Investigation.* Harry Soderman and John J. O'Connell, Funk and Wagnalls Company, New York, 1952.
27. *Municipal Finance Administration.* International City Managers Association, Chicago, Illinois, 1955.
28. *Municipal Police Administration.* International City Managers Association, 5th Edition, Chicago, Illinois, 1961.
29. *The Naked Communist.* W. Cleon Skousen, The Ensign Publishing Co., Salt Lake, Utah, 1962.
30. *Narcotics.* Norman Taylor, Delta Book, New York, 1963.
31. *Narcotics.* John B. Williams, William C. Brown Company, Dubuque, Iowa, 1963.
32. *Narcotics and Narcotic Addiction.* David W. Maurer and Victor H. Vogel, Charles C. Thomas, Publisher, Springfield, Illinois, 1962.
33. *The Penkovskiy Papers.* Oleg Penkovskiy, Avon Company, New York, 1966.
34. *Plainclothesman.* Frederick W. Egen, Arco Publishing Company Inc., New York, 1963.
35. *Police Administration.* O. W. Wilson, McGraw-Hill Book Company Inc., New York, Toronto, London, 1950.
36. *Police Planning.* O. W. Wilson, Charles C. Thomas, Publisher, Springfield, Illinois, 1958.
37. *Police Records.* O. W. Wilson, Public Administration Service, Chicago, Illinois, 1951.
38. *Police Report Writing.* John C. Hazelet, Charles C. Thomas, Publisher, Springfield, Illinois, 1960.
39. *Principles of Management.* Harold Koontz and Cyril O'Donnell, McGraw-Hill Book Company, New York, Toronto, London, ——.

40. *Public Personnel Administration.* O. Glenn Stahl, Harper & Row, New York, 1962.
41. *The Secret Rulers.* Fred J. Cook, Duell, Sloan, and Pearce, New York, 1966.
42. *The Story of Secret Service.* Richard Wilmer Bowan, The Literary Guild of America, New York, 1937.
43. *A Study of Communism.* J. Edgar Hoover, Holt, Rinehart, and Winston Inc., New York, Chicago, San Francisco, Toronto, 1962.
44. *Technics for the Crime Investigator.* William Dienstein, Charles C. Thomas, Publisher, Springfield, Illinois, 1965.
45. *The Worlds Greatest Military Spies and Secret Service Agents.* George Barton, The Page Co., Boston, 1917.
46. *You Can Trust the Communist.* Fred Schwarz, Prentice-Hall Inc., Englewood Cliffs, New Jersey, 1960.

Government Printing

1. "The Challenge of Crime in a Free Society" Presidents Commission on Law Enforcement and Administration of Justice, U. S. Government Printing Office, Washington D.C., February 1967.
2. "Commission on Organization of the Executive Branch of the Government." Government Print, Honorable Herbert Hoover, Chairman Intelligence Activities—report to Congress, June 1955.

Magazines

1. *The American Legion,* June 1967, "Why Do We Need the C.I.A." by Albelt S. Jerrold.
2. *F.B.I. Law Enforcement Bulletin* May issue, 1966.
3. *Readers Digest,* June 1945, "Jump to Adventure."
4. *Readers Digest,* October 1944, "40 Minutes that Changed the War."
5. *The New York Times,* March 12, 1944, "Detective in a Derby Hat."
6. *American Mercury,* April, 1940, "Behind Poland's Defeat."

Other Sources

1. The 1966 Annual Report of the Los Angeles Police Dept. Intelligence Division
2. Pamphlet—A student text—*An Introduction to IBM Punched Card Data Processing.* IBM Corporation, New York.

INDEX